This Book Will
Make You Successful

FERBANE

18 NOV 2021

WITHDRAWN

Jo Usmar

Quercus

First published in Great Britain in 2016 by

Quercus Editions Ltd
Carmelite House
50 Victoria Embankment
London EC4Y 0DZ

A Hachette UK company

ISBN 978 1 78648 143 6
Ebook ISBN 978 1 78648 144 3

10 9 8 7 6 5 4 3 2 1

Editorial and design by Bookworx

Printed and bound in Great Britain by Clays Ltd, St Ives Plc

Contents

Introduction

'Well done, that was a huge success!' You've just wrapped up a presentation to a group of important clients and your boss is ecstatic. According to her it couldn't have gone better. You, however, feel a bit deflated. What about when you had to stop mid-flow in order to sneeze really loudly? Or when the projector started making a strange whining sound and everyone laughed? Or when you pronounced Worcester as War-chester? Besides, who cares about impressing these clients? They're awful, horrible people.

We all want to succeed, but 'success' means different things to different people. It's natural to want to be the best that you can be – but what does that actually mean? Not everyone wants the same things out of life. Success can mean running your own company, raising happy and healthy kids, getting on the property ladder, having a job you love, owning a swanky car – and so on. The options are endless. In today's society, where a job for life and guaranteed yearly pay rises are dusty memories of times gone by, success is no longer determined by just money or power (for most people). At least it shouldn't be. There's so much more to strive for.

According to the *Oxford English Dictionary*, success is 'the accomplishment of an aim or purpose', which is about as vague as you can get. It's hard to read that without musing on nail-biting questions such as, 'But what if I only scrape through by the skin of my teeth?', 'What if I have to screw someone over to get there?', 'What if I don't actually care about accomplishing it at all?' Which is where we get to the nitty gritty of what 'success' really means: achieving something that genuinely matters to you (not to your boss, partner, parents or to society) and learning how to recognise that achievement when it happens.

If you've picked up this book, you probably feel you're not exactly where you want to be in life. Perhaps you want to better yourself in some way, fulfil your full potential, be more appreciated, or steal your boss's job. The good news is that all of these things are infinitely do-able (except perhaps the boss's job thing. But hey, give it a shot). There are key skills and knowledge that, once learned, will help you to achieve whatever it is you want to succeed at – be it progressing in your career or negotiating Christmas dinner arrangements with your in-laws. Which is where this book comes in…

Why choose this book?

This Book Will Make You Successful is a straightforward and practical guide to getting what you want out of life. Using extensive research plus interviews with therapists, career consultants, experienced negotiators and professionals across all fields of expertise, this book will deliver strategies for becoming successful both in work and day-to-day life.

There are tips, tricks and tools detailed throughout that will offer simple and effective ways of achieving your goals. You'll learn how to be more diplomatic, well organised and a good negotiator. You'll master how to both give and receive constructive criticism, how to work to deadlines and know when to ask for help (which isn't a weakness, by the way). There are strategies on how to feel both motivated and motivational, with tips on conflict resolution, building self-esteem in yourself and others and beating procrastination. We'll cover networking, body language and how to stop feeling like a fraud. All these tools will build the regard you're held in by colleagues, associates, friends, yourself and, well, everyone, which will ensure you're treated fairly – and if you're not, you'll know how to deal with the situation effectively (and no, whizzing off a passive-aggressive email is not effective).

This Book Will Make You Successful will enable you to be unafraid of change and of taking well-reasoned risks. You'll feel more willing to stretch yourself, to try new things and not panic about making mistakes. These are skills that will help you in every area of your life, both professionally and personally.

How to get the most out of this book

+ Do the strategies! Don't just skim-read the book and then wonder why nothing seems to be changing. You wouldn't skim-read a manual on deep-sea fishing and then leap onto a trawler brandishing a rod. You'd do your research, learn the skills and practise. Try all of the strategies (identified by **S**); even the ones you think aren't relevant for you. This is a manual for getting what you want out of life and the strategies really do work. Some of them may suit you better than others, but by trying them all and investing time and energy into them you're giving yourself the best possible shot at success

+ Practise. Practise. Practise. Work at it. Do it again and again. Repetition is how we lumbering humans remember stuff. It's the way new habits bed in until they become second nature. It's also the only way you can alter belief systems you've relied on for years – the belief that a certain way of doing things is the right way. Teaching your mind to accept that there may be different, more effective, ways of going about things will take work. It's going to be pretty tough. Sure, there are some strategies within this book that will provide immediate results, but for genuine long-term change you need to work hard. This stuff doesn't happen overnight (sorry!). Minds are stubborn, they need convincing. And the only way to convince them is to practise and take things seriously. Does that sound boring? I really hope not. Because if you truly want something enough you should be prepared to sweat a little for it

+ Please read the chapters in numerical order at least once. You can dip in and out as situations demand after that, but the book is written sequentially, with each chapter building on the last, so missing stuff early on may hold you up later
+ Buy yourself a new notebook specifically for this project. Yep, an actual book with pages you can write on – with a pen. Sounds prehistoric, I know, but writing things by hand has been proven to aid memory, limit distractions and make things seem more 'official' in your head

NB Please note that this book is not about managing money, nor does it provide advice on financial investments of any kind.

While 'success' means totally different things to different people, there are key life skills you can learn that will help you to achieve anything you want, from setting up your own business to having the confidence to go travelling by yourself. Just by picking up this book you've taken the first step on the road to success. As cheesy as that sounds, it's true. You've been proactive in seeking out advice on how to achieve what you want. That's huge! So many people bumble along, not making changes, despite knowing that things aren't progressing as they'd like. This book is your nudge in the right direction. Prepare to feel motivated, productive, influential, effective and, yes, successful!

I

Your Success Story

What does 'success' mean to you? What do you actually want out of life? This chapter will teach you how to set out worthwhile and rewarding goals that you'll enjoy working towards. Because, if there's no satisfaction in it, what's the point in success?

What do you actually want?

Imagine you find a grubby, rusty lamp in the middle of a desert. You give it a rub (because we all would) and a large stern-looking genie wafts out. 'I'll grant you three wishes,' he says in a deep rumble. You open your mouth eagerly to respond and... nothing comes out. All of a sudden you have no idea what you really want. Money, power, popularity, respect, loyalty, fame, love or just some more goddamn free time? You need to work out what, to you, signifies 'success'.

As we have already seen in the introduction, success is a deeply personal thing. What you classify as 'successful', Mike over the road might not give a toss about. You may think you know exactly what you want to work towards, but in reality it's your mum's dream, not yours at all. Thank God, then, that there is no impatient genie hovering over your head and you have a bit of time to consider this vital issue. When it comes to making goals and achieving them, you need to start thinking about what success means to YOU – and you alone. Not what it means to Mike, your mum, cultural tradition or society at large. What will make you feel fulfilled? Here's how to start...

Making SMART-ASS goals

'I want to be rich', 'I want to be a brilliant actor', 'I want to be admired by my peers'. Good for you! Off you go, then! Hang on a minute, though – how rich do you want to be? How brilliant? Which peers? Statements like that sound impressive, but don't actually mean anything – they're too vague. All they do, in fact, is make you strive for an idealised view of perfection that doesn't actually exist. How can you feel successful, or even recognise when you ARE successful, if you have nothing concrete to work towards? This is where SMART-ASS goals come in.

You may have heard of the 'SMART goals' process before (the ASS bit on the end is my own addition). It's an effective guideline to follow when considering what you actually want to achieve in life. It's all too easy to make airy-fairy plans for a distant future that, surprise surprise, never comes to pass. The SMART-ASS mnemonic forces you to sit down and really think about what you want, what you value and what you'll do to get it. Your goals should be:

+ Specific
+ Measurable
+ Achievable
+ Relevant
+ Time-specific
+ Ambitious
+ Scary
+ Satisfying

Specific

This cuts through the 'I want to be rich', 'I want to be powerful', 'I want to be loved' generic guff we often spout to others and to ourselves, but that lead us precisely nowhere. What, *specifically*, do you want to achieve? For example, the following are all specifics: 'I want to earn £6,000 next month', 'I want to secure a speaking part in a film', 'I want to go on a third date with someone I actually like'.

Measurable

This ties in with 'specific' in that every goal should be measurable, so that you'll know when you've achieved it. For example, you'll know if you earn £6,000 in a month, if you get a speaking part in a film and if you go on a third date you enjoy. Replace adverbs that aren't measurable, such as 'great', 'brilliant' or 'best', with details that are quantifiable and which you can actually measure.

Achievable

Right. So this is an interesting one. 'Achievable' means 'realistic' and people driven by success often take umbrage at this: why should goals be realistic? Was Steve Jobs driven by realistic goals? Was he bollocks! And they have a point, but I don't agree with wiping achievable off the goal-making map. There's no harm in aiming high, in fact it's admirable and that's how people achieve amazing, world-changing feats (see 'Ambitious' on the facing page). But they don't just wake up one morning and change the world. They go step by step. And each step they take makes the next step more achievable. It's a process. If your goal is to own a property, yet you have no savings and no idea what the word 'mortgage' even means, then that goal isn't immediately realistic. However, making an appointment with the mortgage advisor at your bank is. Asking property-owning family and friends for advice is. Looking into the price of properties in an area you like is. Starting a savings plan is. Breaking your goals down into achievable steps is an essential part of success. And if you reach a stumbling block, the fact that you've broken the goal down into smaller steps will enable you to see ways of negotiating the obstacle or of taking a sideways route to get there. For example, if your goal was to become a vet, but you discover you're badly allergic to all fur, you could look into working with reptiles or helping the local vet surgery with fundraising rather than dismissing the goal altogether. So achievable stays in. Sorry, nay-sayers.

Relevant

'Relevant' in this context means worthwhile and it's the most important point by far. Whatever goal you start working towards has to mean something to you, otherwise who cares? What's the point? If it doesn't matter to you, then you won't feel any satisfaction in completing it or you simply won't try. Becoming a gardener (even though you feel pretty ambivalent about plants) just because your grandpa was a gardener is a recipe for failure and unhappiness. Similarly, thinking you want to be famous solely because the world venerates 'celebrities', but without considering whether you'd enjoy the intrusion fame brings, is ridiculous. You have to care about your goals; they have to offer a reward you truly value (see the rewards table, page 15).

Time-specific

When will you have done this by? Without some form of deadline many goals and ideas disappear into the ether, reappearing every now and then just to make you feel guilty. When you've broken down your goals into achievable steps, put deadlines on those steps. If it helps, make goals that are initially long-term (years), then work backwards, breaking them down into medium-term (months) and short-term (weeks or days). Seeing a plan like that makes it much less intimidating and suddenly it will appear do-able. Just ensure you note all your self-imposed deadlines in your diary so that they're 'official'.

Long-term (1 year)	Be part-way through or have finished a novel
Medium-term (6 months)	Have a regular writing routine in place
Short-term (3 weeks)	Look into creative writing classes. Write chapter plan
Super short-term (tomorrow)	Write down all my ideas

Ambitious

Don't hold back. Okay, so the world is stress-inducing and competitive and you might fail (which is, actually, a good thing, see page 17). But far better to have had a crack at it than spend the rest of your life wishing you'd at least tried. As long as you break each goal down into achievable steps, nothing should be considered 'too ambitious' at the outset.

Scary

Get scared. Push yourself. Test yourself. Not all stress is bad and we reach our peak performance levels when we feel under pressure (see Chapter 5). It shows you care. If you don't care about something you won't ever feel scared, so you may never hit your peak and never excel at it. Pushing yourself and taking risks means you're learning new things, feeling inspired, motivated, passionate and interested. All of which means achieving what you set out to will be immensely…

Satisfying

Working out what you actually want to achieve, being convinced it's worth it, breaking it down into achievable steps, setting yourself deadlines… and then actually doing it. What could be more satisfying than that?

⑤ Put your goals through the SMART-ASS test

Having read through the mnemonic, jot down some goals in your notebook – things you've always wanted to achieve. It doesn't matter how big or small they are, or how long they may take. Just write them down. Now, put these through the SMART-ASS test, using the guidelines you've just read: are your goals specific, measurable, achievable, relevant, time-specific, ambitious, scary and satisfying? If not, why not? Can you adjust them to make them more interesting or valuable? Can you add in a stage to make them seem less intimidating? Putting your goals through this test will ensure you're on the right road to success.

What will your rewards be?

You need to start thinking about the motivations behind your goals: why do you want to succeed at this? How will you be rewarded? What is driving you? What will you get out of it? This will help to clarify how much you really want something and how far you'll be willing to go to get it.

Rewards table

Goals	I'll be rewarded by...
Write a novel	Becoming a publishing phenomenon
Be an investment banker	Being able to retire at 45
Get married and have kids	Proving my ex wrong
Make more friends	Meeting more people, expanding my horizons
Set up my own company	Proving to myself that I can do it
Open up a coffee shop	Knowing I at least had a go
Become a photographer	Being creative

Ⓢ Your rewards table

Copy the rewards table onto a fresh page in your notebook, listing the goals you've decided you want to work towards in the left-hand column. In the next column list your rewards. What do you hope to get out of that particular goal? Be totally honest. Don't write down what you think sounds good or is in some way noble, like 'I want to fulfil my creative potential' when you actually mean 'I want to make loads of money'. There's no right or wrong answer here and you need to be honest about your motivations for reasons that will soon become clear.

If you're struggling to fill in the table try a simple visualisation technique. Say the goal out loud and picture yourself achieving it. Visualise yourself at the height of success. Imagine everything about the scene: Where are you? Who are you with? What are you doing? What are you thinking? How do you feel? It may even help to imagine what you're wearing, holding or the gestures you're making. Are you making a speech to a roomful of your own employees in your brand-new start-up? Or drinking champagne having secured a massive once-in-a-lifetime contract for your company? Maybe you're looking at all the zeros on your latest pay cheque? Or meeting the group of kids your charitable project recently helped? Whatever it is, write it down.

There are two points to this exercise:

1 Forcing yourself to be honest about your motivations may change how you feel about the goal. If you don't think the reward will satisfy you or you're not proud of the emotions driving you, you may feel it's not actually something you want to pursue. In which case you'll save a hell of a lot of time and angst by trying to succeed at something else instead.

2 You'll be able to remind yourself why you're doing what you're doing when things get tough. Because things will get tough – that's life – and it'll be good for you to be able to look back at this list and go, 'Okay, that's what I'm doing this for. That's what I want. And if I get it, this will be worth it.' For example, when you're mid-way through a 14-hour day with a boss who micro-manages your every second, you can chant under your breath, 'I can retire at 45. I can retire at 45' – if that is what your reward is. If the reward isn't living up to expectations or you figure you're paying too high a price trying to get there, you can reassess your motivations and change your goals.

The eight secrets to success

Success analyst and author Richard St. John believes that there are eight secrets to success. Write these eight words in your notebook, on your phone, in your diary or on a post-it note stuck to your mirror and read them whenever you need a kick up the bum.

1 **Passion.** Love what you do (and if you can't love it, love the rewards it brings you).

2 **Work.** Damn hard. No one gets stuff handed to them on a plate. And if they do, they don't usually appreciate it, aren't very good at it and don't get any satisfaction from it.

3 **Focus.** If you really want something, focus on it.

4 **Push.** Push yourself. Hard. You're going to come up against obstacles, problems and fear. Push through these things.

5 **Ideas.** Be curious, ask questions, solve problems, be open-minded, take chances.
6 **Improve.** Be good at it. Practise. Ask for help. Learn. Hone your skills.
7 **Serve.** Serve others something of value and you'll always be successful.
8 **Persist.** Persist through failure and CRAP (Criticism, Rejection, Assholes, Pressure).

Be prepared to fail

'Success is not final. Failure is not fatal. It is the courage to continue that counts.' Winston Churchill

We live in an era of untold possibilities, one in which we're constantly told we can be whatever we want to be. While there's no doubt that this is positive, it does have the flipside of creating a world in which failure to 'win' or achieve huge things can leave people battling low self-esteem.

Philosopher Alain de Botton explained this very neatly in a TED talk. He mused on how, while living in a meritocracy can motivate and inspire, the theory that those at the top deserve to be there inevitably means that those at the bottom deserve to be there too. This is dangerous ground to tread, for it doesn't take into consideration variables such as illness, accidents, luck or privilege, for example. It makes failure that much more crushing, as if it's a personal flaw. It's not. Failure happens to all of us at certain times in our life. Just look at the positive response Princeton University Professor Johannes Haushofer received after publishing his 'CV of Failures': a document containing a list of degree programmes he didn't get into, funding he didn't receive and rejections from academic journals. His aim was to encourage people to keep going despite setbacks and disappointments. To truly find success you have to anticipate and push through rejection. Think about JK Rowling. Her first Harry Potter novel was turned down by around a dozen publishers before it was finally taken on.

And Brian Acton, who, after being rejected for a job at Facebook in 2009 went on to create WhatsApp, which Facebook then bought for $19 billion in 2014. Imagine if either of them had packed it in after the first 'no thanks'.

Ⓢ Don't take professional rejection personally

Some people like certain things, others don't. That's life. No one's out to get you or is manipulating things so that you'll fail (at least, I'm pretty sure they're not, unless you've got a nemesis – which would actually be kind of exciting). Maybe someone else got the job because they accepted less money, or they know the boss's daughter, or they're more up for travelling for work than you are. Take on any feedback, learn what you have to learn, move on.

Ⓢ Don't be scared to change your goals

Success is fluid, life is complicated and priorities change. Throughout this process, if you find yourself unsatisfied by what you're doing, don't be frightened to reassess your goals. Check over your rewards table and ask yourself: 'Am I still satisfied by those rewards?' If the answer is no, go back and devise new goals. Remember, these days people are likely to have between 12 and 15 jobs in their lifetime, so there's lots of scope for change professionally. Plus, we're all living longer, so our personal lives are bound to encounter swings and roundabouts too. It shouldn't come as any surprise when what suited you at 20 doesn't suit you at 40, and you should expect that what suits you at 40 won't suit you at 60. 'Settling' for something that doesn't make you feel happy or engaged will eventually make you feel frustrated, low and insecure. Taking steps to broaden your life and do things that interest you (whether that's in or out of work) will give you the confidence to make meaningful changes in all aspects of your life. It's as Maya Angelou said: 'Success is liking yourself, liking what you do and liking how you do it'.

Thoughts to take away

✓ Making SMART-ASS goals will put you on the right track for success, ensuring you're making effective plans and that you actually care about what you're setting out to achieve

✓ Be sure of your rewards system – what you hope to get out of the task. If you're in it for the wrong reasons, you'll find no satisfaction in achievement

✓ Don't be scared to fail or make mistakes. Everyone fails at some point. It's what you learn from failure that pushes you towards success

2

First Comes Courage

Self-belief is the driving force behind all success. This chapter will give you the confidence to strive for your goals, knowing you can cope with knock-backs, negotiate obstacles, take chances and grab opportunities.

Everything starts with courage

Success relies on bravery. It's all very well reading strategies on how to be a kick-ass negotiator, but if you're shaking too much to enter the room it's meaningless. Having the courage to put yourself out there, to apply for jobs, to barter better deals, to speak your mind, to take chances and, most importantly, to make mistakes, is the very essence of feeling successful. Courage comes from self-belief, from knowing that you can call on your stores of confidence and self-validation to keep striving to reach your goals – the goals you've just set out in Chapter 1 – despite any obstacles, problems or criticism you may encounter or fears you may face.

'Courage is the commitment to begin without any guarantee of success.'
Johann Wolfgang von Goethe

Why insecurity can scupper your ambitions

A lack of courage speaks to a lack of confidence in your ability to face your fears. If you fear rejection, disapproval, failure or even success, this insecurity can stamp all over your aspirations – and can become a self-fulfilling prophecy when you behave in ways that ensure you don't progress.

A lack of confidence can prompt you to avoid opportunities or sabotage your own chances – rejecting them before they can reject you – which means you never get the chance to disprove your own fears and discover what you can achieve. Building up your self-esteem is an essential part of finding success. Courage and confidence are at the heart of all achievement.

Example: Claire's coffee-meeting crisis

Claire was waiting in a coffee shop to meet a prospective new employer. As a self-employed TV researcher first impressions were incredibly important. Getting on with the rest of the team was essential. If you didn't like each other or respect each other, chances were you couldn't work together. She nervously looked around. A woman wearing a very expensive-looking suit was tapping away on an iPad with perfectly manicured nails at the next table. Something about the woman was familiar. Claire searched for the name of the person she was meant to meet online and clicked 'images'. Oh no – it was her! Claire scowled at her own raggedly bitten nails and faded jeans. Why hadn't she smartened up? Why didn't she have an iPad rather than a phone with a cracked screen? But since when did TV directors or execs wear suits? Did Claire want to work with someone who'd come to a casual coffee meeting in a suit? How pretentious! This clearly wasn't going to work out. Could she leave without the woman noticing? Feign illness? Pretend she'd got the wrong day? No. She was a professional. Claire took a deep breath, walked over, introduced herself and proceeded to act as if she were totally unbothered about the role, answering defensively and even pretty rudely. Unsurprisingly, she didn't get the job. 'I knew it!' she thought.

How CBT can help you to feel more confident

Many of the books in the *This Book Will* series are based on cognitive behavioural therapy (CBT), which is founded on the belief that it's not what happens to you that affects you, it's how you *interpret* what happens to you. This interpretation (your thoughts about the event) affects your body, mood and behaviour. The handy diagram called a 'mind map' (overleaf) has been filled in, using Claire's coffee meeting as an example.

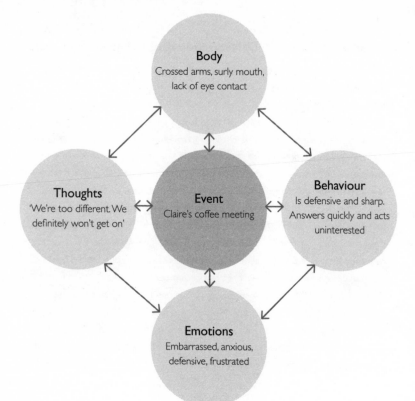

Claire's interpretation of the 'event' (her coffee meeting) is 'We're too different. We definitely won't get on.' This affects her mood, body and behaviour and her actions during the meeting, ensuring that she doesn't get the job – their supposed 'differences' have absolutely nothing to do with it. For all Claire knows they could have got on like a house on fire. Claire let her insecurity and judgement influence her behaviour and therefore scupper her chances. It's Claire's own interpretation that caused the result she most dreaded.

If her interpretation had been more positive, or even neutral, the entire scenario would have played out differently and could have looked like this:

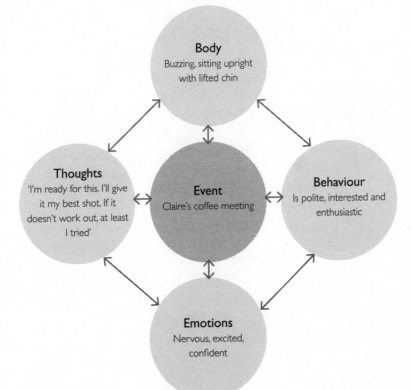

⑤ Fill in your own confidence mind map

Think of a recent scenario where a lack of confidence affected you. Maybe you avoided someone and missed a great networking opportunity, or didn't go on a date because you couldn't face dealing with your nerves. Fill in a mind map detailing what you thought about the event, how your body responded, how you behaved and how it affected your mood. I've filled in another example to help you out.

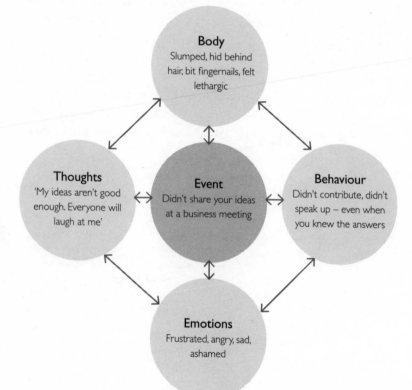

Body
Slumped, hid behind hair, bit fingernails, felt lethargic

Thoughts
'My ideas aren't good enough. Everyone will laugh at me'

Event
Didn't share your ideas at a business meeting

Behaviour
Didn't contribute, didn't speak up – even when you knew the answers

Emotions
Frustrated, angry, sad, ashamed

Can you see how each section influences and, in turn, is influenced by, the others? By changing just one section to positive, the rest will follow. Starting to notice patterns like this – and recognising that you have the power to interrupt them – is the first step towards feeling more courageous about the things you'll have to face to be successful.

⑤ The thought court

The next time you notice a negative thought pass through your head that questions your ability to do something or see something through, catch it and analyse it in this table (see below). Look for evidence both for and against it. You'll probably struggle at first to find evidence against it – your sceptical mind doesn't want you to. It wants you to stay insecure so you stay safe. But that's boring and damaging – so force yourself to do it. Ask yourself, 'Is the thought fair? What skills do I have that might help? When have I achieved something similar before? What would I tell a friend who told me they were thinking this?' (We're always fairer on our friends than on ourselves.)

Thought	Evidence for	Evidence against	A fairer assessment
'My ideas aren't good enough to share. Everyone will laugh at me'	Everyone else always has such great ideas that mine are bound to sound crap in comparison. People laughed at Tom's idea before when they thought it was dumb	No one's ever laughed at my ideas before. In fact, they've already used a couple. Also, someone else gave a similar idea to one of mine when I didn't speak up and everyone loved it	Even if my ideas aren't strong, they're not silly. They'll be jumping-off points for more. And people only laughed at Tom because he'd actually made a joke
'She won't say yes, so why bother asking her out?'	She only dates people who are as into fitness as she is. She also didn't come to the pub when I asked her to join a group of us last week	I'm not a mind-reader. I don't know she's going to say no. And only her ex-boyfriend was into running, I have no idea if that's actually a deal-breaker. She's always really interested in talking to me and laughs at all my stupid jokes	I'll never know unless I ask. Even if she says no it won't be the end of the world. I'll see her at Ed's party on Friday. I can gauge how it's going then

Usually we just accept our negative thoughts as facts, without even questioning them. THOUGHTS AREN'T FACTS. They're just guesses, hypotheses from your nervous brain. As such, they can be challenged. You can step back and ask yourself, 'Well, is that really true?' and try to get a fairer perspective. In just attempting to find evidence against the thought you'll feel more in control as you're being forced to be fairer on yourself.

Confidence dips

Dips in confidence affect everyone at certain times, but if a lack of confidence is severely affecting your life on a day-to-day basis, I recommend you look more thoroughly into the subject. Check out *This Book Will Make You Confident* in the same series. The strategies listed there will help to make you feel able to face challenges, take chances and realise your ambitions.

Appreciate your achievements

Recognising your achievements – and others' achievements – is a crucial part of success. It motivates you to strive for bigger and better things and it fosters empathy and respect. It's not arrogant to pat yourself on the back or swig a celebratory whiskey when you accomplish something you set out to do. Imagine having a sports coach constantly screaming in your ear: 'You're rubbish! You're not good enough. You'll never make it!' Research has shown that constant punishment makes us respond angrily, defiantly or insecurely, while having a coach who focuses on encouragement – 'That was much better! You're doing really well. Keep at it' – gains better results. Give yourself a nod of recognition at passing certain milestones and you'll feel more motivated.

Ⓢ Write down five things you've achieved today

At the end of today, write down five things you achieved. It could be anything from finishing a project to making someone laugh. Nothing is too big or too small. Many studies have shown that writing down a 'gratitude list' – things you're thankful for – boosts positivity and wellbeing long-term. This list is slightly different, focusing more on your own accomplishments – what did *you* do? – but the sentiment is the same and having to acknowledge five things will make you consider the smaller stuff that you might normally brush off as inconsequential. Little things matter and they often get lost amongst the mistakes we make or the disappointments we suffer because those trigger stronger emotions, so are easier to recall.

Ⓢ Create a success pinboard

Have you ever seen a TV programme that pokes around a celebrity's house? There's often a 'vanity wall', or even 'vanity room', covered floor-to-ceiling in trophies, awards and magazine covers of the celebrity's achievements and successes. This isn't egotistical (in most cases), but actually an effective way of boosting confidence and morale.

Make yourself a success pinboard or create a success Pinterest gallery and pin up/post your achievements. Put up photos of moments you're proud of, like the day you were accepted on a course or you finally dumped that chump you were dating. Print out or copy down complimentary emails, texts or tweets and pin up awards you've received – yes, your theory driving test counts. Look at the board whenever you need a confidence boost and remind yourself of all your successes.

Ⓢ Grab your chances and make the most of luck

After university I worked in a pub for the summer. A regular asked what I'd like to do for a living and I said I'd love to work in magazines or TV. He gave me the number of a friend of his who worked in telly. I did nothing for a few days. I couldn't possibly just ring some guy who'd never heard of me and ask for a job… could I? I worked through all the worst-case scenarios (see page 33) and figured the most awful thing he could say was: 'Who the hell are you? Go away and delete my number,' which really wouldn't be the end of the world. So I called him. He was impressed I'd had the bottle to call and asked if I'd do work experience in sales. I didn't know anything about sales, but figured I'd have a foot in the door, so said yes. During my two weeks with the sales team I introduced myself to the studio manager and asked for work experience there too. They said yes and that stint led to my becoming a full-time runner in the Channel 4 studio on a year's contract. And that eventually, a couple of years and different roles later, led to my becoming Channel 4 Commissioning Assistant for Features and Factual Entertainment. All from a casual conversation in the pub.

Have the courage and confidence to grab any opportunities that come your way and to make the most of pure dumb luck.

Stop comparing yourself to 'more successful' people unfairly

There'd be zero point in telling you not to compare yourself to other people at all, as it's human nature – survival of the fittest and all that shtick. The theory of social comparison was first proposed by psychologist Leon Festinger, who identified not only our drive to evaluate ourselves, but how we do it:

Upward comparisons: comparing ourselves to those we think of as better off.
Downward comparisons: comparing ourselves to those we think of as worse off.

When we feel insecure we tend to compare ourselves only to people we think of as better off, measuring our worst bits against their best bits. For example, 'Sarah has such an amazing house, while I live in this grim flat', rather than, 'Sarah has such an amazing house, but I have a better job, so fair's fair.'

Success is getting louder. The pervasiveness of social media means people's achievements are daily documented in technicolour (with a nice filter, of course). There's an actual ranking system for 'success' in how many likes or comments someone's post gets. And this naturally means there's also a ranking system for 'failure' in how few likes or comments a post gets. Measuring your achievements against other people on social media is like diving face-first into an insecurity pit. Remember, people only post statuses and pictures of things they want you to see, not the humdrum mundanity of daily life or the stresses and strains they're under, plus online likes and dislikes have little bearing on the real world. Remember that when you next think, 'I should be like him/her/them'. In real life these people are probably nothing like the way they portray themselves online!

⑤ Only indulge in fair comparisons

Start looking out for times when you compare yourself to others (it can become such a reflex action you don't even realise you're doing it), and then stop and ask, 'Am I being fair on myself and them? Do I know the full story?' Think of Claire's coffee-meeting scenario (see page 23). She compared herself to her potential new employer so unfairly it made her sabotage her own chances. A fair comparison would have been: 'She looks incredibly smart in her suit, but perhaps she'll like the fact I look more laid-back and approachable. Maybe she'll feel uncomfortably overdressed. Maybe she has another meeting straight after this one. Plus, what someone looks like has no bearing on how we'll get on.'

Perfection is bollocks (and quite unappealing)

Perfection doesn't exist. It's a myth perpetuated by your self-abusing brain. That couple with the achingly 'perfect' life on Instagram actually can't bear each other. That 'perfect' guy at work is actually neck-deep in gambling debts. Remember: you never know the full story. You only see what people want you to see. If someone acts as if everything is perfect all the time, they're either lying or are very boring. It's our idiosyncrasies, flaws and shared experiences that make us interesting and familiar.

If you are a perfectionist, might your definition of success be shaped by some societal ideal that you feel you have to live up to or by a voice in your head that ranks your achievements according to an internal barometer of acceptability? Families, friends, colleagues and culture all influence how we judge ourselves and others and that judgement can be fierce. If you don't believe you're 'winning' and think you're falling short of your perfect life plan, you'll beat yourself up and constantly move the goalposts. Yes, you were nominated for that award, but you didn't win it. Yes, you bought your first house, but the kitchen's barely big enough for a toaster. Yes, you had great sex last night, but it wasn't the best sex ever. This is a terrible way to live. You'll never appreciate what you do have or what you've already achieved. Life becomes a constant slog of self-chastisement.

Dwelling on how things should be 'perfect' can make you dissatisfied, competitive, envious and judgemental on both yourself and others. Being perfect is not realistic – or desirable.

In 1966 psychologist Elliot Aronson undertook a 'coffee spill' study in which tapes of a quiz were played to a series of panels. One of the tapes included the 'quiz host' spilling a fictitious cup of coffee over himself at the end. Every single panel rated the person spilling the coffee as more 'likeable' than the others. Many studies have since elaborated on this 'pratfall effect' of likeability and all confirm the same thing: being fallible (and not 'perfect') makes you appear more human, 'normal', easy to relate to and more down to earth. A great example of this is when actor Jennifer Lawrence tripped up the stairs while collecting her Oscar. This is, without doubt, every single person on the planet's worst nightmare, yet she used it to her advantage, laughing about it in her speech and becoming an instant hero to everyone. Which brings us neatly to…

Ⓢ Learn to laugh at yourself

If you're clumsy and fall off your chair, trip up or stumble over your words – laugh. There are myriad studies that prove how laughter makes you feel better both physically and emotionally. Your heart rate picks up, releasing 'feel-good' endorphins that relieve stress and even act as natural pain-killers, making you feel more positive and laid back. By proving you don't take yourself too seriously, you'll come across as friendlier and more approachable; your response allows other people to relax as they'll take your cue in how to deal with the situation.

How to quash worst-case scenarios

This strategy is for every time you think, 'What if?' and your worry grows and grows, until suddenly you're staring into a terrifying abyss of professional and personal doom. For example, 'What if I mess up meeting my new boyfriend's parents? What if I split my trousers in front of them at the restaurant? What if the restaurant has CCTV footage of me splitting my trousers and put it on YouTube? What if I become an international laughing stock? What if I lose my friends, family, house and job? What if I end up living on the streets?'

'What ifs' feed off each other, becoming bigger, uglier and more ridiculous the longer you worry, until soon you've created this terrifying worst-case scenario that seems to predict THE END OF THE WORLD. Why do we believe these thoughts? Because we usually visualise them as we think them – you actually *see* yourself humiliating or disgracing yourself.

You watch the scene play out like a movie in your head. And if you can view yourself doing it, suddenly it seems not only realistic, but likely.

Stop! Most worst-case scenarios are complete drivel, with a sprinkling of codswallop thrown on top for good measure. They come from your terrified mind, which is working against you. It wants you to be scared so that you won't do whatever it is you're contemplating doing; so you'll stay safe, within your comfort zone. This is incredibly damaging, limiting your life experiences and your ambitions.

When you next get caught up in 'what ifs', the first thing to do is notice them. Often they just course through the brain without us even realising it. Just noticing 'what ifs' and metaphorically stepping back from them will immediately give you enough distance to be able to complete this strategy:

⑤ What's realistically the worst that might happen?

Copy down the table below into your notebook and fill it in using a recent example of a 'what if' worry that affected you. I have filled out two examples to help:

What's your 'worst-case scenario'?	'What if my new colleagues think I'm rubbish at my job? What if I am rubbish at my job? What if I fail my probation? What if I never get another job and end up penniless?'	'What if I humiliate myself at the wedding? What if don't get on with anyone? What if all the people I used to know think I'm a failure because I'm single?'
How strongly do you believe this? (0–100%)	100%	90%
Emotions	Scared, anxious	Anxious, ashamed, sad

Behaviour	Don't ask anyone questions, just keep quiet, pretend to work when I actually have no idea what I'm doing	Wear nondescript clothes so as not to draw attention to myself, don't talk much, avoid personal questions
If a friend told you this, how would you reassure them?	Of course you won't know everything – you're new! No one will expect you to. You got the job because you were the best candidate, because you are qualified for it. They believed in you, so believe in yourself	Is everyone who went to your school a bully? No! Also, you LOVE being single so why would that be bad? You've also got a great job and have just bought a flat – you have loads to talk about and be proud of
Now reassess what, realistically, is the worst that might happen?	I won't know what I'm doing for a week or two, but gradually I'll pick it up. I might annoy one or two people with my questions, but they'll understand why I'm asking	I'll have a few awkward conversations with people I never liked anyway (standard at any reunion) and probably have a good time with those I always got on with
How much do you believe the original thought now? (0–100%)	15%	10%

How to stop feeling like a fraud

In 1978 psychologists Pauline Clance and Suzanne Imes identified 'impostor syndrome' as feelings of inadequacy that persist even when faced with information that indicates the opposite is true. In short: when you feel like a fraud. Comedian Tina Fey has admitted experiencing this, thinking, 'I'm a fraud! Oh God, they're onto me!' as has Sheryl Sandberg, Meryl Streep, Sonia Sotomayor and Kate Winslet, while in 1938 John Steinbeck wrote in his journal, 'I am not a writer. I have been fooling myself and other people.'

We all have an inner critic that lives in our heads. A ratty little voice that tells us we're doing it wrong or we're not good enough. It's basing its opinions on beliefs we've long held about ourself, such as, 'I'm not clever/ attractive/sporty/ambitious/likeable enough'. This inner critic is wary of taking risks because it's frightened of the unknown. To challenge yourself is to risk failure and criticism – experiences we associate with negative emotions, so naturally push against them. To maintain the status quo is safe. So when you do take chances or make changes, your inner critic panics, screaming, 'You're not ready for this and everyone will find out!'

The people who tend to suffer from 'imposter syndrome' most are:

✦ Women achieving success in male-dominated industries
✦ Those with high-achieving parents or siblings
✦ Those who achieve success early in their careers
✦ Those who gain a longed-for position or station in life

Research has suggested that women are more susceptible to 'imposter syndrome' than men because they tend to internalise failure. While men will look at external influences, women will find fault within themselves. This doesn't mean it doesn't affect men at all, though, as author Neil Gaiman knows: 'The first problem with any kind of even limited success is the unshakable conviction that you are getting away with something.'

As journalist and author Oliver Burkeman notes, imposter syndrome is suffused in ironies:

Irony 1: You probably don't think you've got it because you believe you're genuinely out of your depth, while others aren't.

Irony 2: This way of thinking suggests that you must be a master of deception to have fooled people for so long. So you ARE super-talented... just at deceiving people.

Irony 3: Trying to cure imposterism through mentorship can backfire as people find themselves lacking in comparison to their mentor.

Irony 4: Getting promoted won't cure it as you'll simply find more scope for feeling fraudulent.

Irony 5: True frauds, idiots and chancers rarely seem to experience it because they don't care about the job or don't care about what other people think. If you do care you're already better at your job than many others out there. So, what can you do about it? Turn to page 38 for strategies to beat imposter syndrome.

Dealing with disapproval

Disapproval is rooted in fear and judgement. We disapprove of things that we'd be scared of doing even if we're not the ones doing them. We also judge people according to our own 'rules' of acceptability, disregarding the fact that different people have different 'rules'.

We live in a cynical world where positive thinking is deemed 'unrealistic'; we expect the worst in a misguided attempt to avoid disappointment and keep 'safe'. This is wrong and very damaging. People who say, 'Are you sure you want to do that?' often aren't making negative judgements on your ability, but are merely voicing those negative-is-best patterns of behaviour. They don't realise that saying 'be careful' or 'are you sure?' is essentially the same as saying, 'I'm not sure you can handle the fall-out if something goes wrong' or 'I wouldn't do it, so you shouldn't'.

Here's news: you CAN handle it. We can cope with so much more than we think. If you have thoroughly researched a plan, know what you're getting into and believe in yourself, ask the doubters to trust you. Don't let fear dictate your life or hold you back, otherwise you'll regret 'settling' (accepting how things are even if they don't make you feel happy, satisfied or fulfilled) and resent both yourself and others for the decisions you didn't make and the chances you didn't take.

🅢 Ask for help

Asking for help when you feel out of your depth doesn't mean you can't cope. See Chapter 9 for strategies that will make you realise that turning to others isn't only brave, sensible and necessary sometimes, but also incredibly liberating. This is especially important if you're thrown in the deep end professionally. If you're new to a job and everyone seems to expect you to know what you're doing, with zero handover notes, you can feel panicky, insecure and, yep, like a fraud. Ask for help. Don't just pretend to type on your keyboard while sweat drips down your brow. Find a friendly colleague and ask for guidance. They probably went through the same thing when they started and will respect you for asking.

🅢 Acknowledge that feeling nervous is totally normal

Feeling nervous about stuff is totally and utterly normal. In fact, it would be weird if you didn't sometimes question yourself – you'd be an egomaniac. Keep asking questions, keep learning your craft and keep asking for advice. And, crucially, keep giving yourself credit when it's due.

Remember: everyone has to start somewhere

Sure, some teenage vloggers have made millions giving beauty advice or discussing computer games while sitting at home in their pants – but they hit the right idea at exactly the right time. Which is rare. Most people have to work their way up and that's no bad thing. It gives you time to learn your craft. It's astonishing how many people sniff at having to do menial tasks when they start out in working life. Making the tea and handing out post is one of the best things you can do when you join a company. You meet everyone from the CEO to the office junior, you get to know them, ask what they're doing and show that you're willing to muck in. Someone has to make the tea and open the post. It's not something to be ashamed of or frustrated by. Don't expect to jump fully formed into your dream job.

Courage and confidence grows from experience. And, in turn, when you have climbed up (success!), don't sniff at the people below you. You were there once (and one day they could possibly be your boss and will remember how you treated them. *Shudder*).

Thoughts to take away

✓ Watch out for how your thoughts influence your body, behaviour and mood. You'll soon notice when things are turning self-destructive or counteractive. You can then stop the negative patterns and replace them with more positive, successful ones

✓ Your gut-instinct 'worst-case scenario' fears are often total nonsense. Asking yourself, 'What's realistically the worst that can happen?' will calm you down and give you the courage to take chances and grab opportunities

✓ Don't dismiss or belittle your achievements. Fostering pride in what you do will give you the confidence to strive for bigger and better things

3

(Net)Work Hard

Is networking really worth it? How do you make, and keep, good contacts? This chapter will show you how to network like a pro, fostering relationships that will successfully lead to job referrals, opportunities and even new friends.

What is networking? Why should you bother?

Networking is building a directory of contacts with whom you share a mutually beneficial relationship. The more people you know, the more scope you have to help people and be helped in return. You can find everything from a new job to a new plumber via your contacts and, in turn, their contacts.

Also, with company budgets stretched tighter than a gymnast's leotard nowadays, many businesses can't afford the process of recruiting in the old-fashioned way: sending out advertisements, going through applications and conducting first, second and often third interviews is a hugely expensive rigmarole. It's perhaps not surprising, then, that many businesses skip it altogether, instead recruiting for up to 80 per cent of their positions in-house or via staff recommendations. The only way to gain access to this 'hidden job market' is to know someone on the inside who can give you a heads-up or drop your name to the right person.

Networking is essential for getting that lucky break, that leg-up you deserve, that position you've earned, or finding a group of like-minded people to share ideas with.

Here's how to network successfully
Give to get

Don't be cagey with your own contacts or knowledge. If you put people together, forward on job leads and make recommendations, people will return the favour. Practising networking in this way will make you feel comfortable with tapping people up when you need tips yourself.

Assess your own value and what you value

Before you call or meet anyone, make a game plan. Enter any meeting with the thought, 'How can I help them? What skills or contacts do I have that they might want?' Assessing your own value will give you a confidence kick, while assessing what the other person, or company, values can give you a clearer idea whether a relationship will work.

Start with your family and friends
The person you most want to meet may only be a couple of phone calls away. You might not know that your mum's friend's wife is a barrister or that your neighbour is a computer programmer. Ask around, then contact them yourself, dropping the mutual acquaintance's name.

Most people have had a stroke of luck or a leg-up themselves along the line and will appreciate the effort and courage it takes to get in touch. Do your research on both the company and them personally and flatter them genuinely. If they think you're serious and they like your attitude why wouldn't they help? (Also, people love being asked to help; it makes them feel good about themselves.)

Don't forget your alumni network
Most schools, colleges and universities have alumni networks and those who sign up to them do so purely to meet and keep in contact with people – hence the name. You'll get an instant directory of useful contacts who won't mind you giving them a shout.

Join professional networking groups
There are hundreds of networking groups you can join, whether they're industry-, gender- or rank-specific (for example, Execunet, IoD, WIBN) or for all professions. The biggest example of the latter is LinkedIn, which has over 400 million members. Signing up to a networking group, attending events and updating your online profile regularly can be a good way to discover who's who and what's happening in your industry. Networking events have an old-fashioned reputation for being stuffy, packed with old guys eating soggy lettuce sandwiches. No longer. There are lots of dynamic

and creative groups that cater for people who want to have a laugh as well as pad out their little black books.

Be sociable

Are there any company pub-quiz teams, parenting groups or sports teams you can join? These are far more laid-back ways of meeting people and getting to know them personally as well as professionally; a great way of making connections that last.

Dress the part if you're attending a networking event

We form our initial impressions of people within the first five seconds of meeting them. We assess their appearance and body language and make a judgement. That judgement can, of course, be adjusted over time, but it's obviously preferable to get off on the right foot immediately. An easy way to do that is to dress the part, whatever that 'part' happens to be. Everyone is different and has their own preferred style, but there are some golden rules that should cover all bases, whatever event you're attending and whoever you're likely to meet:

+ Check out the dress code before you arrive (via other people attending or on the company website) and dress appropriately. There's nothing worse than rocking up in jeans and trainers and finding everyone else in suits or vice versa

+ Dressing 'appropriately' doesn't mean you can't wear something that represents your own personal style. In fact, wearing something bold or special can be a conversation-starter and can make you feel more confident. 'It's good to stand out in the right ways,' Joseph Petchelco, Global Sales Director for Roksanda, says, and recommends going for pops of bold colour, such as a bright tie, piece of jewellery, patterned socks under jeans or a classic simple shift dress, below the knee, in red

+ Dress in something you feel comfortable in. There's nothing worse than being uncomfortable, whether that's physically, if something's pulling or too tight, or emotionally, if you feel too smart, too scruffy or as if you're not representing yourself truly. If you often have to wear suits, but feel too dressed up, replace the shirt with a navy t-shirt and pair with some smart trainers. On the flipside, a stylish pair of shoes with jeans works too

+ Focus on a statement item. Joseph believes that if you're going somewhere people will take notice of your look it's wisest to focus on a good pair of shoes (even if they're trainers) and/or your bag. 'A quality bag speaks volumes even if the rest of your outfit is low-key', he reckons

+ Think carefully through any decision to make a political statement via your outfit. Wearing a t-shirt with an incendiary emblem emblazoned across the front might feel like a grand idea at home, but not so grand when you arrive. Making a statement is fine if that's your entire aim, but it's not the smoothest route to successful networking, which is based on finding shared interests and mutual ground. Also, in business you won't just be representing yourself, but the company; the people you meet have to trust you'll be able to do that. Besides, the statements can come later when you've already built a rapport

+ DON'T WEAR DIRTY OR HOLEY CLOTHES. It's not cool to turn up somewhere with last night's curry down your shirt or a gaping hole under your armpit. If you're careless with your clothes, what else are you careless about? Some people may even see it as a sign of disrespect. If you only notice something like this once you've arrived, reference it yourself before others can: 'I've just noticed the moths have had their way with this jumper. They're naturists at heart'

+ Don't keep your coat on indoors. It looks as if you're waiting for your chance to escape

Beware of your own internal judgements

Jamie was attending a barbecue where he knew he'd meet a guy who worked for a company he admired. He had full sleeve tattoos on both arms and he thought they'd scupper his chances of working at this quite traditional company, so wore a long-sleeved shirt with a long-sleeved jacket, even though it was 30 degrees. He sweated so much he looked ill and couldn't concentrate on any conversations. He finally took off his jacket and immediately bumped into the guy he was trying to impress. 'Is that a tattoo?' the guy asked, looking at his wrist. 'Yeah,' Jamie said, a little defensively. 'They're full sleeves.' The guy immediately pulled up his own t-shirt to show an intricate inking covering his whole chest. In fearing being judged, Jamie had judged someone else. Different people work in different places. Yes, sometimes they won't be into the same things as you, but don't let your own judgements and prejudices cloud a first meeting.

Body language

We all give out non-verbal cues, messages that reveal things about our personality and mood, via our posture, stance and behaviour. Your body language is one of the first things you're judged on and there are simple dos and don'ts to creating an open and approachable impression rather than one that says, 'Stay the hell away'. (Bearing your body language in mind is an integral part of success in all you do, not just networking.)

A study by psychologists at Ohio State University and Universidad Autonoma de Madrid asked people to write down their qualifications for a job. The researchers found that those sitting up straight reported feeling much more confident about their qualifications than those who were slouching. If you feel insecure and scared, faking self-assurance through body language not only makes you appear more confident to others, but actually makes you *feel* more confident.

Body language dos and don'ts

Dos

+ Maintain good eye contact. If this is too intimidating look at the bridge of the person's nose between their eyes
+ Keep an 'open' stance, with your arms by your sides or one hand in a pocket. If you're nervous, hold a glass and rest your other hand in the crook of your elbow – a good way to feel 'safe' without looking unapproachable
+ Keep your chin up
+ Pull your shoulders back
+ Smile. Whatever you do, smile

Don'ts

+ Poor eye contact
+ Look at the floor
+ Hunched shoulders
+ Downturned mouth
+ Rapid eye movement
+ Fidgeting or twitching
+ Clenched fists
+ Biting your nails or picking the skin around them
+ Using body barriers such as crossed arms, a handbag over your chest, covering your mouth with your hand, covering your face with your hair

Don't take your resume or CV to a networking event

Many networking event organisers list this as one of their clients' biggest turn-offs. It smacks of desperation and puts people in the awkward position of having to hold a sheaf of paper at what is meant to be a laid-back meet-and-greet. Just the sight of you standing there clasping a folder in your shaky hands can make people run for the hills. Instead, simply carry a business card with all your contact details on it. It looks professional and is easy to slip into a pocket. Or ask to connect to people on Twitter or LinkedIn. It's a less pressurised way of making a link.

How to nail the perfect handshake and air-kiss

Handshaking

People judge others on the strength of their handshake. It's a fact. The gesture carries a huge amount of influence and, considering people will shake hands 15,000 times in their lifetime on average, it's worth getting right.

+ Always use the right hand. Historically, men would do it to prove they were unarmed. 'Your scabbard would be resting on your left hip, so your right hand would be the one you'd draw the sword with,' etiquette expert William Hanson, author of *The Bluffer's Guide to Etiquette*, explains. So, by putting out your right hand you'd be showing you weren't going to draw

+ Make eye contact. You could have the best handshake in the world, but if you're looking at the floor or over their shoulder you might as well not bother

+ Don't go in with your palm facing downwards so your hand will be on top when you shake. This can come across as domineering and insecure, as if you're trying to show who is in charge, William believes. The palm must face inwards to create a sense of equality.

+ Position the hands mid-way between you both

+ In Britain the handshake should last for two shakes, no more than three, and a maximum of two to three seconds (in the Middle East it can go on for much longer). Hold eye contact throughout and don't break too soon as that may come across as arrogant or uninterested.

+ Use a medium level of vigour. You're not breaking bones here.

+ And finally, practise. Try it out on people who'll give you an honest opinion (so not your nan or the company intern)

·····⋮·

Dealing with shaky or sweaty hands

✦ Use a roll-on antiperspirant deodorant on your palms before the event if you're worried about clammy skin. Just make sure it's one that 'dries clear'

✦ Clench your bum and thighs. The tension will stop your hands shaking

Air-kissing

Air-kissing is now as common as handshakes when meeting people in social situations. It's still pretty uncommon professionally, but not unheard of.

Here's how to do it:

1 If you're unsure what's appropriate, take your cue from the other person. If they stick out their hand, shake it. If they lean in for a kiss follow suit (kisses must be reciprocated, not just received and should never be refused).

2 Lean to the left and present your right cheek to their right cheek.

3 Your cheek should lightly touch theirs.

4 Kiss the air (no smacking-lip noise necessary).

5 Repeat on the left cheek. There are no definitive rules on how many kisses to go for, but two is fairly standard in social situations, while one may be all that's needed if it's professional. Again, follow their lead after the first to see if they lean in for another. If you bash noses, don't panic, just laugh.

Don't fear going to events alone

Yes, it can be intimidating arriving somewhere alone, but it can also be beneficial. You won't be held back by your friend or colleague if they're shy and you won't be judged by their behaviour if they're a pain; you can chat to whoever you choose, rather than getting stuck with someone terminally dull, who your friend wants to impress, and you'll be the first to learn of any new opportunities.

Why chatting in groups is better than pairs

Picture the scene: you're wandering about alone looking like the least-popular leper in the leper colony. You see a similar lonely leper. You join forces. You are now a pair of lepers. Guess what? No one wants to hang out with a pair of lepers. Even if your leper friend is hilarious and charismatic, it's always best to join a group than forming a pair because there's less pressure on you to create scintillating conversation and you meet more people. Individuals in a group feed off each other, bouncing back and forth, so there's more opportunity to listen and learn about the people you're with and interject when you feel ready. In a pair you also risk getting stuck with a hanger-on who inhibits your own networking opportunities. (NB, be aware whether you might be that hanger-on yourself. If you are, scarper pronto.)

Social media: simple traps to avoid

Social media is brilliant for networking, but it's mind-blowing how many people either forget, or don't care, that their social media accounts are public. Potential employers, friends or partners will check them out. There are news stories every month of someone being fired or forced to resign from a great job for a deeply offensive comment they posted online. And, while that's the dramatic end of the spectrum, bear in mind that even writing 'Nailed it!' after a job interview could piss off the interviewer when they check your accounts later. Before you write anything that might potentially offend or annoy someone or that's arrogant, stupid, politically inflammatory, unkind or even illegal, stop and assess whether you're prepared to lose potential contacts and opportunities over it.

How to initiate conversations with strangers

1 If you can, ask the host of the networking event to introduce you. This saves a lot of nerves and hassle. And, if the host is savvy, they'll know who you're most likely to get on with.

2 If it's appropriate (i.e. at a personal party rather than a professional event), ask if you can help take round drinks or canapés. This is an easy way to meet people and creates an immediate talking point, 'Would you like a mini burger? I'm Michelle, by the way.' This also gives you a great excuse to move on if the conversation dies a miserable death.

3 If you can't organise an intro, pick the friendliest-looking group of four or five people. Acknowledge your presence by making eye-contact and smiling. You can then listen for a few minutes before joining in.

4 Alternatively, ask a generic non-personal question like, 'Do you know where the bathroom is?', 'Do you know what time the speeches start?', 'Can I have some of that guacamole you guys are sharing?'

5 A great ice-breaker is to give a genuine compliment (it has to be genuine otherwise it will sound like fawning). Admire someone's outfit, hair, jewellery or gold teeth. A smart tactic is to have done your research beforehand. There is nothing more flattering than meeting someone who has bothered to find out about you. Everyone loves hearing great things about themselves from an unexpected source. 'Hi, aren't you George Smith? I just bought a bag you designed. I love it! How long have you been making them?' 'Hi, Rosie. Didn't you used to work at X? I work there now! They still talk about how brilliant it was when you were there. Tell me some stories.' This also has the added bonus of steering the conversation away from the standard 'Grim weather, isn't it?' boringness that characterises many first-time encounters.

6 Another 'in' is to chat about a shared experience at the event, i.e. a group getting stuck in the lift on the way up, your name tag being spelled incorrectly, the slow bar service or someone smashing a glass.

7 Otherwise talk about an experience that happened to you recently that you believe will strike a chord. For example, 'the trains were running okay tonight, unlike last week when I was stuck for two hours during rush hour with my face rammed against the window'.

8 Always ask open-ended questions that don't demand much effort to answer. So, for example, 'You live in Kentish Town? I've heard it has some excellent pubs. Any recommendations?' rather than, 'What's Kentish Town like?' Another example would be, 'Have you seen the latest movie by John Smith?' rather than, 'Seen any good movies lately?' People don't like having to work at small talk.

9 Listen properly. People often just wait for their turn to talk when the only thing they'd have to do to impress is listen (see Chapter 4).

10 Don't pretend to know something you don't. It's the death-knell of any successful networking experience. You can't blag your way through a conversation about the ecological state of China or a book you haven't read. You'll look like an idiot. Instead say, 'I'm sorry, I don't know much about it. Will you talk me through it?' You'll probably be helping a lot of other pretenders out too and the person you ask will be pleased to wax lyrical about it (unless they're a pretender too!).

Thank the staff

Always be polite and courteous to the staff at any event. Many people judge potential colleagues, job candidates and friends by how they treat people working at a venue.

Don't be swayed by job titles

Sure, it would be great to have a one-on-one chat with the COO of the company you want to work for, but she's currently surrounded by 15 acolytes guffawing at her rubbish jokes. Go and talk to the PA, office manager or receptionist instead. Never underestimate the power of the

A trick to help with social anxiety

If you find it hard to talk to strangers, practise. Start saying 'Hello' to the postman or asking the cashier at the local supermarket, 'Busy today?' It'll get you used to initiating small talk, but without the pressure of having to make a good impression.

diary keepers. They have their boss's ears. They're the people who can get you in and put in a good word. Also, as powerful as the big boss is, they often have very little to do with the day-to-day running of a large company. Whereas, the receptionists, office managers and PAs know everyone, from the post boy to the head of recruitment. Get on the right side of them and you're speaking to the most influential people in the business.

Take action

A subtle way to impress is to take action during an event, for example by offering to get the drinks or taking someone's coat for them. It illustrates decisiveness and proactivity without showing off.

Take the next steps

After you've spoken to everyone you planned to, focusing on what you can do for them and how you can benefit their company (not just chewing their ears off about your own brilliance), ask for their business card and proffer one in return or note down their email address. Always cement the contact before you leave the venue.

Don't dismiss the power of getting a foot in the door

If someone offers you work, a placement or a temporary contract in an area you're not bothered about, but in a company you love, don't dismiss it outright. Being in the building is priceless. You'll look keen, capable and resourceful in seeking out the person you really want to work for, they'll be able to put a face to a name and you're skipping the whole CV-lost-in-cyberspace hell. Plus the fact you're already working in the building means you're probably a safe bet.

Find another way in

Who cares if you don't have the right qualifications or you missed the deadline? Print off a bunch of CVs and start knocking on doors. Call and email people. Get creative. Show them what you can do. Think up unique ways of getting their attention. Do your research. Focus on what you can do for them. Make a personal connection and show a bit of ingenuity. Don't give up. Sure, you may not have quite the right qualifications, but you have tenacity, ingenuity and charm. Use all the persuasive tactics detailed in Chapter 4 to get people onside.

Make your own networks

If there are no groups or events around that interest you, make your own. Email some colleagues and friends and ask if they'd like to meet up on the last Thursday of every month. Tell them to bring some friends. Chances are other people have moaned about the same lack of suitable networks and they'll appreciate your effort in starting something. Also, consider linking the group to something else to spark interest, for example, maybe a pub quiz, a charity event or a book club.

Keep up to date with prospective employers

Careers coach Nancy Collamer recommends signing up for Google news alerts about prospective employers. One bing! on your phone and you'll know if the company has just signed a huge new partnership deal, received additional funding or leased plush new office space – all signs that they might be hiring. If you get an alert about one of the execs weave the flattering information into an email or phone call.

Consider going freelance

Freelancing gives opportunities to meet people from all walks of life and most industries hire consultants in some form. It's the most effective form of networking I know – it's all part of the job. Obviously, there are both pros and cons – the nomadic desk life doesn't suit everyone. You also need some experience behind you before you can start, but if you think you'd relish the freedom and could handle the potential instability, you should look into freelancing within your particular industry. Ask consultants, freelancers or an agency for advice.

Do what you promise

If you commit to putting two people in touch with each other or to looking over someone's resume, make sure that you do it. Empty promises are the kiss of death for successful networking as you can appear to be unreliable, forgetful or, worse, untrustworthy.

Mentors, sponsors and coaches

What are they and how can you get one?

Mentors

Mentors give guidance and advice and can expect the same in return. It's a relationship built on trust and respect and therefore usually grows organically from a connection or friendship. You can't just demand that someone mentors you having just met them. They need to have at least some knowledge of your skills, talents, work ethic and attitude in order to assess your compatibility with them. Mentorship doesn't have to be something that is categorised or set in stone; it's not often you'd have to ask someone to be your mentor – it just happens. You'll likely have several mentors at different stages of your career and you'll probably mentor people in turn. Many companies have mentorship programmes that you can take advantage of, which will try to pair you up with someone compatible. There are also external companies dedicated to finding mentors. However, it's the people who discover a personal connection who have the most success, not those who turn up and ask: 'What can you do for me?'

Sponsors

A sponsor is someone who'll actively endorse you, often without you even knowing about it. Rather than the more holistic approach of a mentor, a sponsor is someone who will use their position to influence things to go your way rather than give guidance or advice. Again, they will only do this knowing your skills and talents. No one is going to put their name on the line for someone they don't know.

Coaches

A business coach is like a sports coach; someone who is hands-on, helping develop your specific skills, giving constructive criticism, helping goal-setting and suggesting ways to work better. There are companies who hire consultant coaches or you can look into hiring one independently.

Thoughts to take away

✓ Networking is a two-way street. Help others and they'll help you; always go into any meeting having prioritised how you can help them, rather than how they can help you

✓ Don't undervalue the importance of first impressions. Dressing well and exhibiting positive body language can be the difference between successful or unsuccessful networking

✓ Be bold, brave and tenacious. Don't be scared of hearing 'no' – there's always another way in

How to Get What You Want

Getting on the right side of people can get you what you want – and it is ridiculously easy. Never underestimate the power of politeness, respect, integrity and a good attitude. Being pleasant and interested in other people is all it takes to be persuasive – and persuasiveness is an essential tool to utilise in your quest for success.

Persuasion: more powerful than force or manipulation

If I said, 'Meet Sally, she's very persuasive…' it doesn't sound particularly positive, does it? It sounds like Sally's a bit crafty; that she's pretty adept at getting people to do stuff they didn't originally want to do. Which is unfair because Sally's not like that at all. She's pleasant, interesting, an excellent listener and a damn good saleswoman (Sally's not her real name – she persuaded me to use a pseudonym).

Persuasion absolutely isn't manipulation if you're basing your proposals on reason and good sense and, here's the most important bit, are willing to be persuaded another way yourself. And that's the golden ticket to effective relationships: having the humility to admit that you don't know everything and believing that other people's opinions and needs matter. Success in life depends on it.

Sure, psychopaths have traits that can make them excellent business folk – ruthlessness, egomania and a distinct lack of empathy being just three – but they're not first on anyone's dinner-party guest list or known for their long-lasting business relationships. The non-psychopaths among us have to learn how to muddle along together. The following tips will enable you to handle yourself (and others) in an effective, attractive and influential way – essential skills to securing success in any endeavour.

Remember people's names

It's a magnificent gift to have a memory for names because it makes you instantly likeable. Your name is your identity; it's what separates you from the crowd and what makes you YOU. If someone forgets your name (or doesn't make the effort to remember it in the first place), it feels as though you yourself are forgettable, not interesting or important enough to remember; ergo you immediately take offence at the forgetter. Remembering people's names is a skill many successful politicians and celebrities credit with their success. Also, in today's digital world, where names are instantly available at the touch of a button, people are getting lazier at remembering personal details in 'real life'. So recalling a name when face-to-face can set you apart in a positive way and pave your way towards long-term success.

Ⓢ The name game

Quick tricks to remembering names:

1 Repeat the name out loud straight away: 'Nice to meet you, Chris'.
2 Say it three times in your head: 'Chris, Chris, Chris'.
3 Make an instant connection: 'Chris has curly hair and looks like my old teacher'.
4 It's even better if the connection rhymes: 'Chris likes to fish'.
5 Or if it's alliterative: 'Chris works in computers', 'I met Chris at Christmas'.
6 Ask straight away if there's something about their name you're not sure about (better than asking the fourth time you meet). This is particularly important if you are unfamiliar with the name itself: 'Do you prefer Chris or Christopher?' or 'Sorry, could you remind me of the pronunciation again?'

What to do if you forget the person's name:

+ If you forget the name immediately, ask at the end of that first conversation, but start with a compliment to soften the blow: 'It was really lovely to chat to you, but I'm terribly sorry, I've already forgotten your name – my brain's like a sieve'
+ If you see someone approaching and think, 'Oh God, I should know that person's name, argh! What is it?' ask the person you're with who hasn't met them before to step in. For example, you (Caroline) ask your friend (Luke) to jump in with, 'Caroline is being so rude, she hasn't introduced us. I'm Luke. And you are?'

✦ Style it out, if appropriate: 'Hello, love/lass/mate/pal/dude/sir/ madam. How are you?' (Think on Zsa Zsa Gabor, who once admitted, 'I call everyone, "darling" because I can't remember their names'.)

✦ Fess up: 'I'm terribly sorry, your name's totally escaped me. Please remind me?'

What not to do. Ever:

✦ Attempt to escape from the situation by pretending you can't remember having met them before and so re-introduce yourself. This is a million times worse – you're not only suggesting that their name's forgettable, but that their entire self is forgettable

✦ If you do genuinely forget having met someone before, so re-introduce yourself and they correct you, quickly find an excuse for your lapse in memory: 'Of course! I'm so sorry! Have you changed your hair? Were you wearing glasses last time?' Both you and the forgettee will be relieved to find a reason for your forgetfulness

The email name game

If someone's email address contains the full name Jessica, but they sign off as 'Jess', address them as Jess. Jessica is fine the first time (how were you to know until they'd replied?), but not the second or third. Acknowledging how they refer to themselves shows you've paid attention and are placing importance on their name, thus on them as a person. Don't ever under-estimate the importance people place on their own names – especially if their name is part of their business, for example Dan's Motors. If you start your email to Dan of Dan's Motors with 'Hi Daniel', he'll think you're a plonker.

Always smile

Smiling is a universal sign of welcome and approachability. It crosses all divides: racial, geographical, sexual and cultural. It defuses discord and douses rage. It both physically and mentally makes you feel better. (Studies have proven that just the act of smiling can make you feel happier, just as feeling happy will make you smile.) Success involves dealing with people and that's always easier if you smile. Think on the old Chinese proverb: 'A man without a smiling face must not open a shop'.

If you have a face like thunder no one's going to want to hire you, buy from you, sell to you, ask for your help or generally talk to you at all. 'Who cares? I'm the boss. I don't want to talk to anyone', you might think. That attitude will cause a general sense of unease to filter through the ranks, resulting in longer-term problems. The thought, 'Yeah, but you don't have to deal with the cretins I do every day,' may also cross your mind. True. But said 'cretins' may only be cretinous because they're scared of, or don't like, working for you. Changing your attitude is the first step in changing theirs. You're not too busy or important to smile.

A 30-year longitudinal study at UC Berkeley found that students who displayed genuine smiles in their yearbooks had lower divorce rates later in life. This makes sense when you consider that smiling can reduce stress hormones while increasing endorphins and lowering blood pressure. A 2010 Wayne State University study found that smiling can even extend your life. Researchers examined baseball cards of Major League players from 1952. Players who didn't smile lived an average of 72.9 years, while those with big, honest grins lived an average of 79.9 years. Additionally, a Penn State University study found that when we smile we not only appear more likeable and courteous, but also more competent.

Ⓢ Smile, even when you don't feel like it

When all you feel like doing is crawling under your desk and swigging some gin, slap a smile on your face. Smiling stimulates the brain's reward system, with one smile having the ability to provide the same level of stimulation as eating 2,000 chocolate bars or being given a wad of cash. It mentally and physically changes how you feel. Anger, fear, grumpiness, insecurity or defensiveness won't get you far in business or your personal life, so when you know you're walking into a stressful situation, a grin is your best armour.

Ⓢ Smile once an hour

Put an alarm on your phone to go off once an hour to remind you to smile. And then do it! It won't just make you feel better – other people will feel better too. Smiling really is contagious. Humans are biologically programmed to mimic smiles as an evolutionary process of evaluating how genuine a smiler is and the emotion behind the gesture.

Ⓢ Smile when you're on the phone

Sure, the person on the other end of the line can't see you… but they can *hear* you smiling. Researchers at Portsmouth University found that listeners were able to identify Duchenne smiles on the phone – smiles that raise both corners of the mouth and the cheeks and also form crow's feet.

Say thank you

So much angst, bad feeling and misunderstandings could be avoided by two simple words: 'thank you'. According to philosopher and psychologist William James, 'The deepest principle in human nature is the craving to be appreciated.' Some people find appreciation in money. They get paid well so don't care if their boss barely acknowledges their existence (see Rewards Table, Chapter 1). But what about when they get home – if they

Example: Jonny's jobs

Scenario A

Jonny's email: 'Hi, please find my work attached. Thanks for this commission. I really enjoyed it. Hope you like it.'

Jonny: 'Hi. Hope you're well! I haven't heard anything from you. Just wanted to check you received my work and you were happy with it?'

Jonny: 'Hi there. I still haven't heard from you so am assuming you've received the work and are happy with it. Please find my invoice attached.'

Editor A: 'That's not the amount we agreed on.'

Jonny: 'I think you'll find it is. £2,000 + £400 VAT, as I'm VAT-registered.'

Editor A: 'That's fine. You hadn't explained you were VAT-registered. I didn't know.'

Scenario B

Jonny's email: 'Hi, please find my work attached. Thanks for this commission. I really enjoyed it. Hope you like it.'

Editor B: 'Got it! Thanks so much for the speedy turnaround. We really appreciate it. I'm looking forward to reading this. I'll give you a shout with any questions. Meanwhile, please ping over your invoice.'

Jonny: 'Great! Thank you. Please find my invoice attached.'

Editor B: 'I'm so sorry, Jonny, but I think you've put the wrong figure on the invoice. I believe we agreed £1,500?'

Jonny: 'Yes, we did! Sorry, I should have explained. I'm VAT-registered, so the extra £300 is the 20% VAT.'

Editor B: 'Of course, that makes perfect sense! Thanks again for the work. I really liked it. We'll definitely be calling on you again.'

then do all the gardening, washing, cooking and cleaning and never receive a 'thank you' or 'great job' for that either? When you take things for granted they can easily fall apart.

If you were Jonny, who would your rather work with: Editor A or Editor B (see box on previous page)? Even though Jonny earns less money when he works for Editor B, he prioritises their commissions because they appreciate his work and have a pleasant attitude. Sometimes gratitude is more important than financial reward. As filmmaker Kevin Smith said, '... and the dude never even said thank you. Never once said, like, "Hey, thanks for taking the time out". That's a big thing with me. I'll do anything as long as somebody says, "Hey, thanks". Gratitude is a big part of my life.'

⑤ Don't dismiss the power of 'thank you'

+ Say thank you when someone does you a favour. Many people will hold a grudge if you don't show appreciation when they've gone out of their way for you. It's just plain crappy

+ Say thank you when someone completes a task, even if they're simply doing their normal, everyday job. Also, make sure to say it when they haven't done particularly well. If the only thing anyone ever hears is criticism or silence, their work will suffer, while receiving praise will motivate them to do better

+ Say thank you to those at home. Appreciation is about being valued personally, showing that you care and noticing what others do. Remember: as soon as you start taking things for granted or believing people don't deserve recognition for certain things, resentment builds

Thanks is the definition of getting something for nothing. In this case the 'something' is respect, pleasure and good will.

Shut up and listen

It's the simplest trick in the world: if you want to be successful, just listen. Stop talking in a loud, shouty voice, trying to impress your view on others, and listen. Then ask pertinent questions. The most successful people are all listeners: people who don't just want to inject their own two pennies' worth into every conversation or prove how clever they are, but who are honestly interested in others. Everyone is flattered by being listened to because it happens all too rarely these days. We're all so busy and wrapped up in ourselves, it's a big compliment if someone sets aside time for you. If you want to get on in life, quash your desire to be loudest, funniest and smartest and let someone else have a go. Listen to them instead.

Listening not only gets you off on the right foot with people, it's the foundation of every good decision you make. What do other people want? What are they looking for? Why are they angry? Why are they acting this way? We're all so caught up with getting our own points across, we forget that people generally don't disagree with us, provoke us or behave atrociously for no reason. Most people just want to be heard. Listening douses anger, provokes meaningful discussion and will earn you major brownie points.

⑤ Are you listening?

Check in with yourself next time you're in a conversation with someone: are you listening – really listening? Or are you monopolising the chat? Or are you just waiting for your turn to speak? If you had to quantify how much everyone's contributing to the conversation in percentile points, how much would yours be? 70 per cent? 80 per cent? Aim to get it down to less than your fair share – so if there's two of you, try talking less than 50 per cent for a while and instead ask more questions.

Ⓢ Don't multitask

We're crap at multitasking. Don't let anyone tell you differently. You can't concentrate on all the tasks fully, so you end up completing all of them half-heartedly. Multitasking is especially troublesome when you're mid-conversation – when someone's chatting to you, but you're half-reading the news at the same time. They suddenly ask, 'What do you think?' and you have no idea what they're talking about. Listening properly not only boosts concentration but aids memory. If you're constantly forgetting things or can't remember people having told you important facts, you're not listening. You're wasting other people's time and making them feel unimportant. Stop multitasking and you'll notice your relationships, work and attention span all improve. (You'll also get more stuff done: multitasking is not an effective way of being productive. See Chapter 9.)

Ⓢ Don't interrupt with something that's off-subject

Someone's just started on this great story. It's building up and up to what's inevitably going to be a killer punchline. Wait for it… 'Hey! Anyone want a tea? Everyone got enough notepaper?' you shout. Everyone looks at you. The story-teller stops mid-flow, completely bemused. This kind of interruption is usually triggered by nerves, but that doesn't make it any less rude. Control yourself and wait until the other person has finished their story, even if you do have a valid point to make.

How to talk persuasively

We can exert a lot of influence over people by our linguistic choices:

Ⓢ Talk in terms of the other person's interest

This is one of Dale Carnegie's focus points in his epochal book *How to Win Friends and Influence People*. Based on the belief that people only really want to hear about themselves, he recommends opening a sales pitch with what you can do for the other person rather than with how great you or your products are. Ask yourself, 'How can I get them to want to do this?' and proceed accordingly. For example:

'Dear Mr Sykes. I know you currently use a car-based delivery service. My motorbike courier service will dramatically decrease your delivery times as bikes can nip in and out of city traffic. This will reduce your overall costs and increase customer satisfaction. As we'd like to secure your business, we offer you a 10 per cent discount for the first month.'

Rather than this:

'Dear Mr Sykes. My motorbike courier service has just celebrated its fifth birthday (who cares?): five years of stellar service and happy customers (says who?). Recently we were proud to win the contract for new business development in Stratford (anything to do with me?)...'

⑤ Banish certain phrases from your mouth

Never say, 'Why don't we?', 'Why can't I', or 'You didn't... did you?'. 'Why don't we?' is usually followed by a positive suggestion such as, 'Why don't we go to the pub?' or 'Why don't we go away this weekend?', yet framing the statement negatively invites the listener to actively look for reasons why you shouldn't. It's the same with genuine questions: 'Why can't I have a pay rise?' will prompt your boss to defend their decision not to give you one. Far better to use proactive and positive phrases instead, such as, 'Let's go to the pub!' or 'I'd really appreciate a pay rise; I believe I've earned one'. (On the pay-rise note, don't ask, 'Can you explain your reasons for not giving me a rise?' Again, you're inviting your boss to defend their decision and list your faults. Don't give them the chance. Instead ask, 'What more can I do to prove I've earned a rise? When can we meet again to discuss it?')

The construction, 'You didn't… did you?' (as in 'You didn't buy that car, did you?') is a slightly different case in that it casts pre-emptive judgement on the answer. You'd never ask this unless you already knew the answer was most probably 'Yes, I did'. In which case you've left the listener in no doubt as to your opinion on the subject: a big fat thumbs-down. 'You're not going to have a big traditional wedding, are you?', 'You didn't accept that job, did you?' What a terrible position the person you're asking is now in! They can't win and will have to defend their decision – a decision which is probably none of your business anyway.

⑤ Don't correct people if it's unnecessary

No one likes a smartass, no one likes to be told they're wrong and no one likes to look stupid. These three universal facts of life mean that if you correct someone unnecessarily they will defend themselves (even if they know they're wrong) and you will get into an argument. If you then win the argument, you'll have made them look stupid and you'll have made yourself a new enemy. So what have you really won?

Example: I couldn't care less

David: 'And then in *Midnight Cowboy* Jon Voight improvised, shouting, "Hey! I'm walkin' here! I'm walkin' here!"'
Tommy: 'Voight didn't say that, Dustin Hoffman did.'
David: 'What?'
Will: 'Jon Voight didn't say that. Dustin Hoffman did.'
David: 'No he didn't. Voight did. I studied film at university.'
Will: 'No, you're wrong. I'm sorry, but it's a fact – Hoffman said it. It's one of his most famous quotes. Sarah, wasn't it Hoffman who said that?'
Sarah: 'I honestly couldn't care less.'

If you don't have to correct someone – if their mistake isn't going to affect business or end the world – then just keep quiet. You'll only alienate them and make yourself look petty. Also, don't bring someone else into the debate as you're only extending the circle of shame for whoever's in the wrong. (Also, never correct someone's grammar in public.)

⑤ If you do have to correct someone...
If the mistake will affect things or people in a meaningful way, tactfully suggest it might be wrong: 'Oh, I thought it was 2009, not 2005. I may be wrong, though. Shall we look it up?' This way no one loses face.

⑤ Don't ridicule others
If you believe someone has done something silly or been taken for a ride, don't make fun of them. Our fear of being ridiculed makes us react defensively, even if we know you're right. For example, which Bill do you like more in the following scenarios? In Scenario B (see page 72), because Bill didn't ridicule Kate over a potentially sore subject (the price of her new car), she admitted her worries to him anyway because she felt he might then be able to reassure her. Self-deprecation and a willingness to admit fault creates a feeling of camaraderie and safety. Ridicule and superciliousness does exactly the opposite.

⑤ Get someone to say 'yes, yes' first
Get someone to say 'yes' twice first, before you pitch them a proposal and they're more likely to say 'yes' again because they're already on a positive thought trajectory. It's a persuasive technique that Dale Carnegie confirms works as a great influencing tool. For example, 'Didn't we have a wonderful time on holiday last year?', 'Yes, it was great', 'Wasn't it brilliant escaping real life for a bit?', 'Yeah, so relaxing', 'Shall we go to Barcelona next weekend for a little holiday?', 'Hell, yes!'

Example: Which Bill is more likeable?

Scenario A

Bill: 'Is that your new car out front?'

Kate: 'Yes! Do you like it?'

Bill: 'Sure. How much did you get it for?'

Kate: '£3,000.'

Bill: 'How much?! Wow, they saw you coming!'

Kate: 'What?! I actually thought I got a really good deal.'

Bill: 'Yeah, sure you did.'

Kate: 'Cars of that age and mileage usually go for twice that.'

Bill: 'It's best to get someone who really knows about these things to check it out for you first.'

Scenario B

Bill: 'Is that your new car out front?'

Kate: 'Yes, do you like it?'

Bill: 'Sure. Looks great. Love the colour.'

Kate: 'Thanks. I actually think I paid slightly over the odds for it, though.'

Bill: 'Oh really? Buying cars is such a pain. I don't blame you for wanting it, though.'

Don't dismiss other people's ideas

I worked in an office where regular ideas meetings would often end badly. And we all knew why. A senior member of the team would cut people's ideas down stone-cold without debate, leaving them either too scared to share or talking over each other as they defended themselves. Sentences like, 'That won't work because…' or 'They've already said no to something like that' left people frustrated and angry. When people are undermined they'll feel less confident putting ideas forward again.

Ⓢ Remember: ideas are born of ideas

Even if the original idea isn't exactly right, where's the harm in working through it and finding something new from it? Shutting things down before they've had a chance to grow is short-sighted and counter-productive.

Ⓢ Saying 'no' stifles creativity/makes people feel threatened

Words like, 'no', 'won't', 'don't', 'can't', 'didn't', create a negative atmosphere that subconsciously gets people's backs up. When people feel threatened they go into fight or flight mode – they shut up or get aggressive – which means you can kiss any effective brain-storming goodbye. Instead try, 'Okay, let's take this aspect and run with that a bit – see where it gets us'.

Ⓢ Let someone think that the idea is theirs

Pride has a lot to answer for in difficult relationships. Our desire to come out on top is inbred, as is our desire for recognition and appreciation. Which means that if we come up with a potentially award-winning, parade-worthy idea we want everyone to know about it. But people respond better to ideas they've had a part in creating. This is particularly relevant when the idea will affect them directly.

Imagine this: your boss calls an all-staff meeting and crows, 'I've had the most wonderful idea! We're all going to start work at 6 a.m. and finish at 2 p.m., rather than start at 9 a.m. and finish at 5 p.m. Isn't that great? It means we'll be able to work better with our international partners and get home earlier.' Wait, what? Hold on a goddamn tiny minute. No one consulted you about this. What about the effect on your life? Who does your boss think he is? You must stop this plan at all costs.

Whereas, if your boss had called a meeting and asked for suggestions on how best to deal with working across different time zones, you may have all come to the same conclusion eventually anyway – but together.

You'd have felt much less antipathy towards the idea if you were at least consulted first. And, if the boss was really clever, he would pre-empt the criticisms himself and get you to find the solutions. For example, asking you all to think of creative ways to deal with childcare issues, perhaps by introducing a company nursery or flexible working. People are more likely to find positives in a new plan if they feel they were given a choice and/or had put some personal investment into the decision.

⑤ Give credit when and where it's due

Don't ever take credit for someone else's work, undermine them or brush off their achievement. You'll only create bad blood and distrust. Giving everyone their proper dues breeds positivity, motivation and creativity. You're never losing out because someone else had a good idea – there aren't a finite number of ideas to be had in the world. Their new idea will most probably create more opportunities (and successes) for you too.

Know your value

Follow these three bits of priceless careers advice:

1 Act as if you matter
2 Know your own value
3 Become more valuable

I Act as if you matter

If you act as though you matter, people will assume that you do matter – they'll take it as a given. If you act as if you don't matter, people will assume you don't. So, ask to attend meetings, speak up, share your ideas, set daily goals, ask to be included on round-robin emails, go to after-work drinks and place personal items on your desk so you feel you belong (even if you're a temp). If you feel bored at work, ask yourself: what would you do if you mattered? People who think they truly matter are rarely bored.

2 Know your value

Every so often, check in with yourself: what are my skills, what am I bringing to this relationship/job? Could I be doing more? If the answer is no, it's perhaps time to move on as you clearly feel you've learned all you can from your present situation. If the answer is yes, move on to point three (below).

3 Become more valuable

You will always be successful if you add value to people's lives; if you are providing a service that people want and need. If you want to be more appreciated, to be better paid, to get a promotion, ask: 'How can I be more valuable in this situation?' Success comes from proactivity, from a desire to learn and take action. This will make you feel more valuable to others and to yourself. We want to feel useful – if you don't, then make yourself useful.

Email etiquette

You can't avoid using email (unless you're super-rich and have someone who does all your correspondence for you) and there are some basic rules to follow that will see you safely through any potential e-nightmares.

E-greetings

+ The personal touch goes a long way. Refer to the person within the email: 'I wanted you to be the first to know, Beth'
+ Don't use nicknames or terms of endearment for people you don't know as it comes across as condescending, for example, 'Hi lovely'. Equally, don't project a personality onto somebody either, like 'Hi trouble', as they may find it offensive
+ Don't initiate putting a kiss on an email if you're unsure about it, just reciprocate if they send one first. However, don't at all if you feel

uncomfortable about it and be wary of sending one to someone you've never met as it can seem sycophantic

✦ If you send a kiss in error, quickly send a follow-up email (as if you'd forgotten something) without a kiss. They'll realise the first was a mistake or not even notice it at all

Private practice

✦ Don't use your office email account for personal mail. Someone sitting in a dusty underground office will be reading all your dirty secrets. Your work emails are not private. They are officially company property and can be retrieved and used against you if anything goes wrong legally

✦ Don't have a casual moan about a colleague on email. This may come back to haunt you. If you want to make a complaint, keep it formal as your email will be referred to if the complaint is taken further

✦ Don't bcc someone in unnecessarily. You'll lose control of who sees what

Don't hit send

✦ Don't get suckered into an e-argument. Ask to meet face-to-face. Emails can't convey the conversational nuances – you can't read body language or hear inflections so it's easy to take things the wrong way

✦ Most servers have an option to delay messages in the setting menus. Activate this if you regularly deal with personal information or important people so you can cancel an email quickly if you accidentally send 'No, you can't have a pay rise, Amy' to the whole office

✦ If you do send something in error, don't hit 'recall'. Rather than recalling the message this just sends another email flagging up how you don't want the first one read. Whoever received it will automatically then want to read it

+ If you're sending something terrifyingly important, save it in drafts and take a five-minute break from it before re-reading it and double-checking the 'To' box
+ Never send an email in anger. Wait. Calm down. In half an hour you'll probably feel quite different about the angle you want to take
+ Only use 'reply all' if it's relevant to everyone cc'd in and if you need collective input
+ Don't ignore the 'reply all' button if it's needed. It's infuriating for the recipient of your email if they then have to re-send it to everyone else

Watch what you say
+ Watch out for spelling mistakes on group emails – it looks lazy. Run it through a spell-checker or quietly read it out loud. Reading out loud gives you a chance to hear what you can't see, which is a clever way of noticing misspellings or omissions
+ Don't try to be funny unless you're sure you've got the right audience
+ Don't use slang or abbreviations even if someone else in a group message does. A VIP may be reading it with a seriously disapproving look
+ Beware of using only uppercase letters as they appear shouty and may come across as aggressive. It's the difference between, 'Don't worry about emailing me back' and 'DON'T WORRY ABOUT EMAILING ME BACK'

Own up to your mistakes with style and panache

Mistakes happen. Sure, they're frustrating and often annoying, but not all bad. They can inspire creativity, personal growth and innovation, leading you to learn more about yourself and others. Penicillin, chocolate cookies, microwave ovens and even cornflakes were all created from mistakes or by accident. It's how you deal with mistakes that marks you out: dwelling on them and becoming insecure and defensive – or learning from them.

⑤ Admit to your mistakes when you know you should

If no one will ever find out about your mistake and it won't affect others, by all means keep schtum. But if others do know and it does affect them, don't try to shift or share blame or pretend the mistake never happened. You'll look like a fool and appear untrustworthy too – and if people don't trust you, they don't respect you. You can kiss success goodbye.

People respect those who take responsibility for their actions. Imagine this: your brother turns up to an important family meal late and flustered. He drinks too much too quickly, doesn't eat anything and then blurts out the important news you'd been planning to reveal together: that you're setting up a joint business using your gran's inheritance. Your mother and father get upset that you didn't discuss this with them first and a huge row ensues. As you leave, your brother snaps, 'I knew this dinner was a bad idea – it's all your fault. You always have to do everything your way.' You're left wondering 'Do I really want to go into business with him?' Imagine how different things would be if, after the argument, your brother had said, 'I'm really sorry about that. I was stressed and tired. I shouldn't have blurted the news out. I'll call them tomorrow and apologise.' You'd still be pissed off, but you'd feel mollified by his apology and his determination to fix things. Your future working with him would look a lot better.

⑤ Accept apologies and mind your own business

If someone owns up to their mistake, accept it and move on. If you don't believe you've had an adequate response, speak to them privately (not in front of others). If the mistake has nothing to do with you, mind your own business; don't demand an apology on someone else's behalf. If you believe someone has been hard done by, speak to the 'victim' and find out whether they'd like you to step in. If they would, use the strategies in Chapter 6 that detail how to bring up difficult subjects effectively.

⑤ If all else fails when you've cocked up, think on this

'I think there's something a bit weird about people who arrive fully cooked, completely sorted, get everything right first time,' Danny Dyer, says in his book *Life Lessons from the East End*. 'I didn't, but I wouldn't have wanted to. They say you ain't a jockey until you've fallen off ten times, and if you're a motor racer who never crashes, you ain't going quick enough. Life's like that. Take my advice, don't take my advice. F**k things up a bit, life gets interesting that way.'

An added bonus of owning up to your mistakes...

...is that it really takes the wind out of people's sails. If you know you've done something wrong, launching in with a stringent critique of yourself before anyone else can will leave them gaping like guppies. It's also a hell of a lot more fun than trying to defend yourself.

Thoughts to take away

✓ Always listen. It boosts your concentration, aids memory and flatters the hell out of whoever you're listening to

✓ A few linguistic tricks can make the difference between having a row or having a laugh, getting a pay rise or getting nothing, making friends or making enemies

✓ Admit to your mistakes. It's admirable, courageous, trustworthy and takes the wind out of angry people's sails

5

Stress: Success's Nemesis

We all deal with stress on a day-to-day basis, but how you cope with being put under pressure can set you apart from the crowd. Knowing how to stay calm and level-headed will make you more focused, approachable, competent and therefore successful in both your personal and professional lives.

Stressed to kill?

Nowadays we're expected to be all things to all people – all the time. You have to be the highest earner, the best cook, the greatest parent, the life and soul of the party, the gym nut, the health freak, the shoulder to cry on, the generous host, the dutiful child – the list is endless. We're also expected to be available every waking moment via our phones, computers and tablets. No wonder 'stressed' is a state we're all familiar with and one in five people in the UK report feeling anxious 'all or a lot of the time'. Feeling on edge or under pressure sometimes is totally and utterly normal, but if you're experiencing it every single day or know deep down (in that miserable place where self-truths fester) that you don't deal with stress at all well (some might even call you a 'stress-head', although not to your face), it can affect how you view and work towards success. Do you recognise any of the following symptoms?

+ Making excuses as to why you can't do things ('I'm too busy', 'I've got too much on', 'I can't deal with that right now')
+ Often feeling angry, irritable, fearful, ashamed, guilty, defensive, insecure or frustrated
+ Becoming easily distracted and finding it hard to concentrate
+ Poor time management
+ Difficulty making decisions
+ Becoming reckless
+ Colleagues finding you hard to work with
+ Friends mentioning that you seem uptight
+ Constantly seeking reassurance from friends, family or peers
+ Either working too hard or not hard enough
+ Increased drinking or drug-taking
+ Over- or under-eating

Experiencing any or all of these things will inhibit your ability to realise your ambitions and be successful in both your professional and personal lives. If you're snappy, irritable, reckless, uptight or hiding in your room, yours isn't going to be the first name people think of when a job opportunity arises or when a spare ticket to Glastonbury goes begging.

Stress is an emotional and physical response to being put under pressure by a situation or event. It's a natural part of life. If you try new things and push yourself, you will experience stress. That's a fact. You can't ban stress or get rid of it – and nor should you want to. It's your body's way of flagging up a change in tempo, a change in pressure. Your heart starts racing as your blood starts pumping and your body gets you ready to take action. So, while the word 'stress' is usually used negatively in everyday language, it can actually be really positive – and lead to success.

Humans perform well under pressure – when your body's buzzing, your mind's racing and you feel totally engaged. This kind of 'good stress' is reliant on your caring about the outcome – caring about hitting that deadline, making a great speech or impressing the right people. If you don't care about a challenging task, you won't feel stressed about it and you won't get any satisfaction from completing it. The level of achievement you feel upon completion of a task will be relative to how bothered you are about the task in the first place. It's the feeling you get while waiting to go on stage when you know all your lines and are confident you're going to excel at your performance. It's the thrill you get when you're about to walk into a bar to meet a date for the first time. It's the flip your stomach executes when you're about to pitch a great new project to your boss.

We're built to withstand a certain amount of tension. In fact, we thrive on it. But there is a tipping point; a point at which good stress turns bad.

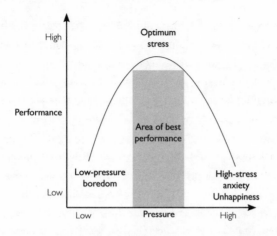

This graph shows the progression from 'bubbling along nicely' to 'possible explosion'. Where 'buzzing' turns to 'freaking out' and thoughts like, 'Okay, I can do this, let's go!' turn to 'Woah! I can't do this, I must shout at people really loudly'. When stress gets too much, it can turn into anxiety: a fear of failure or a perception of threat or danger. And when that happens, fight or flight arrives and the gates of mayhem are flung open.

Fight or flight
(aka feeling like you're going to throw your computer out of the window or hide under your desk)
When stress reaches a pitch that causes proper anxiety you'll feel 'threatened' and your fight or flight reflex will be triggered. Your sympathetic nervous system floods your body with adrenaline and cortisol, initiating a process of dramatic physical changes. This is part of our inbuilt survival system and it's one of our most primitive human traits, dating back to when we were all a lot hairier and ate woolly mammoths for breakfast. You'll recognise the symptoms: increased heart and respiratory rates; increased sweating; hyper-alert senses (pin-sharp vision,

supersonic hearing and a stronger sense of smell). Blood is redirected from fingers and toes and non-essential combat organs like those that deal with digestion (which can make you feel nauseous) and pumped into muscles that need it for fighting or fleeing instead. This means you might literally get 'cold feet' or tingling fingers. Blood vessels in your skin even constrict to ward against excessive blood loss so you'll look pale and clammy.

And that's not all. Your rational thoughts disappear. They bail. They go MIA. You're in attack mode, your body primed to either fight or run, so you don't have time to be rational. Being analytical will only get in the way. Your body knows this and so ditches brain for brawn.

Fight or flight was designed to protect us from saber-toothed tigers and the like, and the trouble is, it hasn't evolved much. Your body still reacts the same way to any sense of danger, whether physical or psychological – it can't differentiate. So, fight or flight will kick in whether your boss throws a bin at you or fires you – great in the first instance (you can dodge the bin), but not so helpful in the other (sweating, shaking and losing ability to think rationally).

Nowadays our daily lives can be so frenetic and stressful that our bodies are constantly in fight or flight mode and never get a chance to calm down. Usually, once 'danger' has passed, the parasympathetic system kicks in, releasing noradrenaline to reverse the changes. However, constantly living 'on edge' means that the process never reaches that stage and so you end up being permanently tense. This is incredibly bad for you, both physically and mentally. Physically, it can cause dizziness, hot flushes, headaches, nausea, stomach cramps and stop you sleeping. Mentally, everything becomes a potential threat. You are biologically primed to look for danger everywhere and so, when in fight or flight mode, you'll find insult, competition and criticism in the most innocent places and either start sniping at people, making snap judgements, behaving aggressively, rudely or insularly (fight). Or hide away, not speak up or not question decisions, rather turning focus onto something else – work, socialising, drink, drugs or food – or isolating yourself (flight).

Here's an example mind map illustrating this horror show (see opposite). This example taps into our tendency to believe that just because we do things a certain way, other people should behave and feel as we do. They don't and won't. Different people live by different 'rules'. We're not all the same. Much of our stress stems from judgemental thoughts such as, 'But I wouldn't do that', if someone upsets you. Because you wouldn't do it the fact that someone else has feels like a personal insult. You have your own standards of behaviour. Other people have their own standards. Accepting this difference will mean that you stop taking things personally.

In the example, because Nina wouldn't play drums at 10 p.m. herself she assumes her neighbour knows it's annoying and must be doing it deliberately. She's taking it personally, so feels threatened and fight or flight kicks in. She either 'fights', reacting aggressively and making the situation worse, or 'flees', not saying anything but getting increasingly wound up by it. Because her rational thoughts aren't working, she doesn't stop to think, 'Why on earth would my neighbour deliberately want to upset me? Isn't it more realistic to think she's probably just being thoughtless?'

Learning to recognise the symptoms of fight or flight will enable you to stop them before it's too late and you find yourself chasing your neighbour down the street with a broom. Calming your body will coax your rational mind out of its hiding place, so you can assess the situation rationally. Our responses can become so ingrained we switch to autopilot and don't realise how our behaviour and mood affects others and how they view us. In Nina's case if she recognised the symptoms of fight or flight and put in place strategies to calm down she'd recognise that it might be more effective to ring the neighbour's bell and politely ask her to stop drumming. If she said no, she could try to negotiate ('Can you start at 8 p.m. and finish at 9 p.m.?'). If the neighbour said no again, Nina

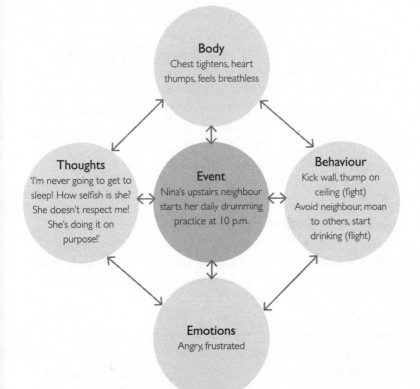

Body
Chest tightens, heart thumps, feels breathless

Thoughts
'I'm never going to get to sleep! How selfish is she? She doesn't respect me! She's doing it on purpose!'

Event
Nina's upstairs neighbour starts her daily drumming practice at 10 p.m.

Behaviour
Kick wall, thump on ceiling (fight) Avoid neighbour, moan to others, start drinking (flight)

Emotions
Angry, frustrated

could ask another neighbour to back her up or call the council. Whatever she did and however it played out, these options are a million times better than acting aggressively or doing nothing.

Learning how to douse fight or flight means you can engage your rational brain and choose how you want to behave rather than have the primitive cave-person within choose for you. This will make you feel in control, so you behave in more competent, effective ways – essential for success in whatever you're trying to achieve.

Anxiety disorders

If anxiety affects your day-to-day life to the extent that you're constantly feeling on edge, physically and emotionally, and are worried about things that don't warrant it, you may be suffering from an anxiety disorder. If this sounds familiar, you should speak to your doctor about further treatment.

Ⓢ Fill in your own stress mind map

Fill in a mind map of a recent occasion when you felt stressed. Recall the physical symptoms: when was your heart racing, your breathing ragged and your chest tight? While thoughts like, 'I can't do this' can whizz through your mind unchecked, the physical ramifications of stress are impossible to ignore. Filling in a mind map will flag up your personal responses to stress and anxiety, so you'll recognise negative patterns in future. I have filled out an example opposite.

Calm down your body and fire up your rational brain

Calming down your body when you feel anxious is essential for achieving success. So before you hit send on that enraged email or stamp on your partner's favourite hat, do one or all of these strategies so you'll be able to consider the issue calmly and rationally.

Ⓢ The intense stretch

When we feel stressed many of us tense the muscles in our neck and shoulders, hunching and 'tightening' up. Master Yoga teacher Lilias Folan of Yoga International believes this is an unconscious attempt to 'brace' ourselves against trauma – real and imagined – for example, when you're being shouted at by an irate driver. This tension triggers negative thoughts, moods and actions (like swearing back) so noticing it and then working to

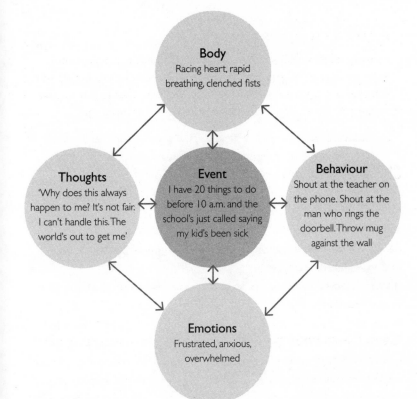

relax is a fundamental step in tackling difficult situations successfully. Follow Lilias' stretch below whenever you notice your shoulders up by your ears. It's called the 'three Rs':

+ Sit tall, with your shoulders down. Tilt your head to the right. Rather than bringing your ear to your shoulder, consciously extend and elongate your neck into the space to your right. The opposite shoulder and side of the neck will lengthen as well. Hold for three breaths. Return your head to centre. Repeat on the other side

+ Now do the three Rs:
  1 **Resist.** Reach your right hand over your head until it rests above your left ear. Use this hand as a 'wall'. Press your head gently into your hand and your hand into your head. Resist gently for three breaths, without moving.
  2 **Relax.** Stop pushing, relax, breathe in deeply and then exhale.
  3 **Restretch.** Softly use your hand to guide your head a little further into the space to the right. Lower your hand and hold for two or three breaths. Return your head to the centre.
+ Repeat on the opposite side and observe which side is tighter

Ⓢ Deep breathing

Do this simple deep-breathing exercise whenever you feel that tell-tale anxiety-induced heart-skitter.

+ Make yourself comfortable. Make sure your legs are hip-width apart and your feet flat on the ground, whether standing or sitting
+ Breathe in deeply through your nose and out through your mouth
+ Count steadily from one to five on both inhales and exhales. If you can't reach five don't worry, just count up to three
+ Rest your hand on your stomach and feel it rise as you breathe in and sink as you breathe out
+ Continue for at least a minute or until you feel calmer

Ⓢ Splash your face and wash your hands with cold water

This is a great idea for two reasons:

1 Because to reach a sink, chances are you'll have to leave wherever you currently are. Even if whatever you're feeling stressed about has nothing to do with your environment, moving will help to clear your head.
2 Cold water can calm the physical effects of fight or flight by reducing your body temperature and 'shocking' your rational mind into action.

How to recognise your own stress triggers

You might think you know exactly what stresses you out (Ian in Accounts, right? Such a jerk), but there could be lots of triggers you haven't considered. You might be so used to feeling stressed that you don't even notice the little things that rile you. By identifying them you can work out how to either cut them out of your life or work around them.

⑤ Keep a stress diary

Copy the table on the next page into your notebook and then fill in the columns each day for one week (only Monday and Tuesday are shown in the example) whenever you feel stressed. It will help you to identify your short-term stressors. At the end of the week look over what you've written:

+ Are there recurring themes? Do you find yourself most stressed at home, at work or when you're trying to go to sleep? Is it usually at a specific time of day? Is each incident related to a particular thing or person (i.e. to a certain project or to Ian in Accounts)?
+ Is there a pattern to how you react to the triggers? Do you usually shout at your computer or storm out of the room?

Finding common patterns to your reactions will shed light on repeat stressors. I asked 30 people to fill in a stress diary for a week. One participant explained she hadn't realised how anxious she felt whenever she spoke to her mother on the phone. Her mum would, without fail, ask her when she was next going to visit (even if she'd only just been) and it made her feel guilty and flustered. Another participant noticed that all of his anxiety surfaced when he was at his desk, but that it didn't always concern work issues. Instead, the constant drilling from the construction site over the road was insiduously ramping up his blood pressure. Someone else revealed how their anxiety reached a pitch at about 3 p.m., no matter what they were doing... but only when they'd skipped lunch.

Your stress diary

	Monday	Tuesday
What happened?	My boss sent me 14 emails overnight	My friend called me and asked if she could stay for a few days after her break-up
Who was I with?	My colleague, Lizzie, who received no emails at all	My husband and our two-year-old daughter
Where was I?	At my desk	At home
What was I doing? (Include the time of the event)	Logging on for the day at 9 a.m.	Trying to get my daughter to bed at 7 p.m.
What was my mood?	Stressed and angry	Guilty, overwhelmed
What were my thoughts	'I knew this would happen! Why does he always pick on me when Lizzie does nothing all day?'	'I barely have enough time at home with my family as it is – now I have to have a sad friend here too?'
How did I feel physically?	Riled up, tense	Tired
What did I do?	Then scowled at Lizzie when she offered me a cup of tea	Said yes even though my husband asked me not to
How stressed did I feel on a scale of 1–10 (with 1 being 'not at all' and 10 being 'incredibly')	8	10

Working this out enabled all three to start navigating their individual stressors – things they hadn't even realised were contributing to the pressure they felt daily. The first respondent booked in regular visits with her mum so they could both stop worrying. The second asked his boss if he could move to a desk away from the construction site and the third started eating lunch every day, no matter how busy they were.

Being proactive about tackling stress will make you feel more in control and better able to cope with frustrations, obstacles and long-term stressors because you're not letting day-to-day things provoke you. This will leave you in a better mindset to fully focus on succeeding at your goals.

Risky business

When you feel stressed it's all too easy pass up opportunities for success, dismissing them as 'too risky'. Where others see options and chances to succeed, you see potential danger and chances to fail. You make excuses: 'I have too much on' or 'I can't afford to take that risk'. You state these thoughts as facts, without questioning them and then write off potentially life-changing choices that could lead you to success. Don't let stress dictate what you can and can't do.

ⓢ Stop using the word 'risk'

The dictionary defines 'risk' as 'a situation involving exposure to danger'. Wow! The word alone suddenly makes whatever it is you're considering doing frightening, when in reality it's probably not. Words have immense power over how we view things and our ability to cope with them. 'Risk' (and 'risky') suggests danger and the possibility of unpleasantness, so by using this word to describe a situation you'll straight away be looking for reasons not to do it. This is particularly true if you then start throwing in the words 'can't', 'must'/'mustn't' and 'should'/'shouldn't' too, which suggest external restrictions you have to abide by. 'It's too risky, I shouldn't do it' is the death-knell for potential opportunities.

The next time you think of something as 'risky' or someone else calls an idea a 'risk', re-name it 'opportunity'. That will change how you view it. You'll be more open to seeing positives as well as potential negatives and to assess choices fairly. Also swap the words 'can't', 'must'/'mustn't' and 'should'/'shouldn't' for the more empowering 'could'/'can' and 'would'/'will'. For example: 'It could be really great working with Julia, I'll look into it'.

S Will you take the opportunity?

1 Write down the decision you're pondering, then draw a line down the page with 'pros' written on one side and 'cons' on the other.

2 List all the potential pros and cons you can think of about taking this opportunity (or not). See the example on the facing page.

3 Put a star next to the points that mean the most to you in both columns.

4 How many starred pros are there versus cons? If there are more pros – hurrah! Stop wasting time dithering and get on with it.

5 If there are more cons, or if the cons are still holding you back, work around them. For example, if you starred 'Not being able to afford my mortgage' could you speak to the bank about a different repayment plan? Do you have savings? Could you launch the business via crowdfunding? Could you seek sponsors from local businesses?

6 Consider whether some of your cons might actually be pros. Is 'Having reduced stability' really so terrible? Might it actually be exciting, challenging and force you out of your comfort zone? Isn't the mundanity of your current set-up part of the reason you want a change?

It's understandable if you decide to prioritise security over passion, but don't let that hold you back from being involved in something you love. If you're not ready to leap feet-first into something, look into taking small steps: invest in a project you believe in, do freelance work on the side, set up an Instagram account dedicated to the subject and see where it takes you. This could be your route to success. If you have self-belief and a bloody good plan there are no such things as 'risks', just new opportunities. Challenge your fears, accept failures, manage your stress levels, prepare to work hard and you'll be well on your way to success.

Decision: Quitting my job to start my own business

Pros	Cons
Doing something I've always wanted to do	Not being able to afford my mortgage
Being my own boss	Not enjoying it as much as I imagined
Choosing who I work for and what I do	My family not wanting me to do it
Keeping my own hours	What if I fail?
Making something that's 'mine'	Having reduced security
Getting to think creatively	Having to work crazy hours to start with
Potentially making my business a success	Having to curtail my spending habits

Thoughts to take away

✓ Fight or flight is the body's natural response to anxiety. Recognising the symptoms and using strategies to calm down will keep you level-headed – and all successful people have to maintain a level head

✓ Don't assume everybody abides by the same 'life rules'. This will stop you taking things personally so you can approach them more rationally and astutely instead

✓ Learning your own personal stress triggers will give you the opportunity to either cut them out or work around them so you stop feeling overwhelmed and can direct all your energies into forging ahead with your plans

6

How to Deal with Conflict, be Diplomatic and Get People to Talk

The worlds we live in (both personal and professional) succeed or fail on our ability or inability to hold important conversations. This chapter explains how you can feel confident when approaching tough talks, how to speak candidly and kindly, and how to encourage open and effective dialogue in others.

The importance of talking – even when it's the last thing you want to do

'I ignored it, I hate arguments', 'I can't believe you just did that to me!', 'I'm just making sly digs at him, hoping he'll realise what's wrong'. Sound familiar? All classic ways of dodging or blundering into difficult situations. And what do they solve? Nothing. Nada. Zilch. Big fat zero. If you ignore the issue or don't address it directly, it will only continue, getting bigger, uglier and more pressing until you're ready to explode with the injustice of it all. However, if you scream the house down and go on the attack, whoever's on the receiving end will instinctively either counter-attack or go into hiding. Either way, nothing is solved. Yet, knowing this, why do so many of us still either run away or lash out when faced with crappy situations? Because we assume any conversation about it will inevitably be a conflict, confrontation or argument. We think that when tackling tough topics there are only two options available to us: be candid OR be kind. Never both. This simply isn't true. The authors of the seminal book *Crucial Conversations* call this the 'fool's choice' because they believe it is totally possible to be both candid and kind. That you can deal with toe-curling chats in effective ways.

The ability to talk – and to talk meaningfully – is fundamental to finding success in both our work and day-to-day lives. Every relationship is founded on the conversations that we do have and the conversations that we don't have; on what is said and what is not said.

The ability to say what we mean effectively is integral for success in every single aspect of our lives, from marriage to business, friendships to families. Here's how to deal with conflict, be diplomatic and get people to talk.

Sharing what you know and what you think you know

Whatever the situation, you need to be open to hearing from others. People make better and more educated decisions the more information is

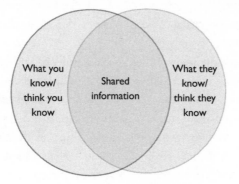

on the table. No matter how much you think you know, other people have a right to be heard, just as you do. Conversations only become effective when everyone shares and feels that they can share. However, there are lots of things that can stop this free flow of dialogue...

Dialogue-killers

+ **Fight or flight** When in fight or flight (see Chapter 5) our brain can only handle two choices: attack or hide. Which means we either turn aggressive and defensive or silent and surly. And then, when we've calmed down, we'll defend our actions: 'I was only saying what everyone else was thinking' (fight), 'He never listens anyway, so what would be the point?' (flight)

+ **The desire to win** This is part of our genetic makeup (that whole survival-of-the-fittest shtick), but it's also a lesson drummed into us from childhood: the quickest, cleverest, sharpest and funniest kids are often the most praised and the most popular. We want to be those people. We want to win

+ **The desire to punish** If someone is being a jackass and you know they're being a jackass, then they should just admit it and apologise, right? Well, what if they don't think they're being a jackass? Shouting at them isn't going to change their mind and it's definitely not going to encourage them to open up

✦ **A desire to keep the peace** When you keep quiet because it's too much hassle or you don't want to kick the hornet's nest, you'll feel resentful. This resentment will then turn to anger and frustration when nothing changes – but, of course, nothing's changing, because no one knows you want it to! You then resort to sarcasm or explode in rage and appear totally unreasonable (and possibly a little unhinged) because to everyone else your fury appears from nowhere

First, check in with your motives

Have you ever had a conversation that starts as one thing and ends up as something else entirely? It's the conversational equivalent of striding along a lovely leafy street only to find yourself suddenly neck-deep in quicksand. Sarah and Mark's conversation about Friday night's plans (below) has spiralled into a relationship-busting chat about general grievances and long-simmering resentments. Their motives changed from 'making plans' to 'winning and punishing'.

Example: Friday night confusion

Sarah: 'I'd really appreciate it if you're friendly to Alex when we see him on Friday, even though he's a pain in the ass.'

Mark: 'Friday? Alex? What are you talking about? We're going to Ricky's birthday party on Friday.'

Sarah: 'No we're not, we're going to see Alex.'

Mark: 'No, we're going to Ricky's. I told you about it.'

Sarah: 'No you didn't. You absolutely didn't. And I told you about Alex's weeks ago. See? It's even on the calendar.'

⋯⋰

....:.

Mark: 'You know I never look at that calendar! Besides I know I told you about Ricky's because I remember discussing getting him a present.'

Sarah: 'You always do this! You always make out that I'm the forgetful one when you never tell me anything.'

Mark: 'But you are forgetful. That's not my fault.'

Sarah: 'Okay, where and when did you tell me about Ricky's?'

Mark: 'Don't be crazy! You always get so irate when you know you're in the wrong.'

Sarah: 'Don't do this – don't patronise me and get all high and mighty!'

Motives in conversations change all the time. They can even turn a totally neutral chat between strangers into a row. For example:

Example: A row between strangers

Customer 1: 'Excuse me, do you think I could pay for my coffee first, please? It's just I'm in a rush.'

Customer 2: 'Hey, we're all in a rush.'

Customer 1: 'But my car is parked on a double yellow; I might get a ticket.'

Customer 2: 'Well, that's not my problem. I have to hurry back to the office.'

Customer 1: 'I don't know why you're being so unreasonable about this. I did ask politely.'

Customer 2: 'Well, you seem to assume that your time is more valuable than mine. Which it's not.'

Customer 1: 'No I don't. You're being stupid.'

Customer 2: 'Hey! Don't you call me stupid –'

Barista: 'While you two have been arguing, three people have paid for their coffees.'

The customers' motives changed from paying for their coffees to arguing over whose time was more valuable. Customer 2 felt disrespected and so went on the attack, prompting Customer 1 to attack back. In both these examples, the people in conversation turned to 'fight', but could just have easily turned to 'flight'.

Fight versus flight in difficult conversations

Symptoms of fight:

+ Talking over the top of everyone else
+ Dismissing people's contributions verbally
+ Dismissing people's contributions physically (i.e. shaking your head or rolling your eyes)
+ Shouting in order to make oneself heard or as a means of intimidation
+ Exhibiting physical signs of aggression: clenched fists, hooded eyes, tensed jaw
+ Calmly arguing your side, without listening to anyone else, until the other person gives in
+ Using personal slights and generalisations (i.e. 'You're being stupid', 'You're sexist')

The result: you get a reputation for being hard to deal with. People don't trust you to hear about their ideas or their side of the story.

Symptoms of flight:

+ Avoidance: refusing to talk at all or steering the conversation to 'safer' issues
+ Withdrawing physically: by leaving the room or using body-blocking mechanisms such as crossing arms, covering the face or mouth

⋯⋰

◌

+ Masking: revealing opinions in cutting, ironic, convoluted or derisory ways i.e. via sarcasm, couching or sugar-coating

The result: either people don't know there's a problem or they do but don't know what it is, in which case they'll feel defensive and turn to fight or flight themselves.

The Motive-Change Vicious Circle:

Both people's conversational motives change

Person A turns to conversational fight or flight

Person B feels threatened, undermined or disrespected

Person B also turns to conversational fight or flight

Stopping the Motive-Change Vicious Circle

People become aggressive or retreat into silence when they feel scared, threatened, disrespected, undermined or angry. Learning how to identify this in yourself and others will stop the Motive-Change Vicious Circle. You have to learn how to fight the natural tendency to defend yourself and also learn how to deal with this tendency in others if you want to be able to have constructive chats about difficult things. And the simplest way of doing that is by identifying your own bad-dialogue behaviour cues using the basics of a mind map:

+ What are you thinking?
+ How do you feel physically?
+ How do you feel emotionally?
+ How are you behaving?

🅢 Your motive-change mind map

Fill in a mind map with a recent time a conversation got out of hand or moved in a direction you didn't expect or want. Often the easiest place to start is with your body as you'll now recognise the symptoms of fight or flight. Is your heart racing, are your fists clenched and muscles tensed? Then check your behaviour. Are you raising your voice, being sarcastic or rolling your eyes? Now your mood. Do you feel threatened, hurt, angry, sad, frustrated, furious or embarrassed? (Pinpointing your exact mood is an integral part of identifying your motive – are you looking to defend yourself, punish others or 'win' the conversation?) And what are you thinking? i.e. 'He's trying to make me look stupid in front of my boss! I'll show him…' Check out the example mind map opposite.

In a situation like the one described, imagine you decide to register your displeasure at the person who asked you to make tea by fuming at your desk and making snide asides for the next couple of days (flight). Your colleague has no idea why you're being rude and so starts avoiding

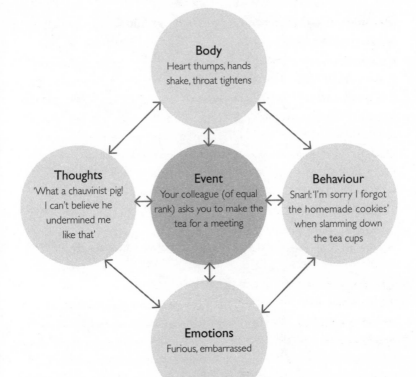

Body
Heart thumps, hands shake, throat tightens

Thoughts
'What a chauvinist pig! I can't believe he undermined me like that'

Event
Your colleague (of equal rank) asks you to make the tea for a meeting

Behaviour
Snarl: 'I'm sorry I forgot the homemade cookies' when slamming down the tea cups

Emotions
Furious, embarrassed

you, leaving you off emails and out of meetings (flight). This makes you angrier, until one day you snap: 'You're just an egotistical moron!' in front of the entire office (fight). He then shouts: 'I told you she was irrational!' (fight) and you feel like screaming. All of which could have been avoided by a calm conversation. By filling in the mind map you'll start to recognise your own emotional cues, meaning that you can also start recognising them in others: 'They clearly feel threatened. What's the best way to deal with this?'

Questions to ask when you recognise conversational fight or flight symptoms in yourself

+ What do I want for myself?
+ What do I want for others?
+ What do I want for the relationship?
+ Am I going the right way to get it?

By asking these questions, you're jolting your rational brain back into action, which will wind down the effects of fight or flight. Remember: the more you care about something, the worse your behaviour during a conversation is likely to be.

The question to ask when you recognise conversational fight or flight symptoms in others

+ Why would a normal, decent person react this way?

Okay, so everyone's different and some people are idiots, but there will always be a reason why someone reacts to a situation badly and it'll usually be because they feel insecure, undermined or threatened. Ask yourself why that may be and if you have anything to do with it. Have you changed your motive? Are you being disrespectful at all? The only person you can control in a situation is you, so if you really want to get somewhere *you're* going to have to take the first steps to making the conversation safe again.

How to get back on track

A Apologise, if appropriate
B Use a do/don't statement to fix misunderstanding
C Compromise OR find a new purpose

A Apologise, if appropriate

In difficult conversations a genuine apology can make the difference between a successful chat or a full-blown brawl. If you've made a mistake or led others to doubt your respect or commitment, start with an apology: 'I'm sorry I didn't tell you that we'd all have to work this weekend. You've worked so hard for the last three weeks I can understand you need a break. This will be the last compulsory weekend shift before the project is finished. I apologise. I should have let you know.'

If this doesn't re-establish a level of calm, or if an apology isn't appropriate, move on to B.

B Use a do/don't statement to fix misunderstanding

A 'do'/'don't' statement is designed to clear up misunderstandings that are either the result of intentional bad behaviour (fight or flight) or unintended misinterpretations of intent. 'I don't want you to think I'm picking on you or ignoring revision you've already done. You've been studying so hard: we're all very proud. I do just want to check you're sure you want to go on holiday and won't feel under pressure when you get back.' The 'don't' comes first as it's the most important bit. You're establishing safety and quashing previous or future misunderstandings.

C Compromise OR find a new purpose

If two people fundamentally disagree on a plan, assuming that compromise is the best way forward can lead to trouble. For example, Tom wants to move to Manchester to be close to his dad, who is ill. His wife, Helen, wants to stay in London because of her job. They compromise on moving to Northampton, from which they both have long commutes and where they don't know anyone, so this doesn't work for either. When a compromise doesn't work, consider looking for a third choice that might suit everyone. Focus on long-term goals: What is more important? What do you value more? Can Helen find work in Manchester? Could Tom's dad move to London? Could Tom move up for part of the week for the time being?

Everyone's three favourite 'it's not my fault or responsibility' stories

There are three types of stories that we tell to justify our behaviour in dealing with tricky conversations.

+ **Victim stories:** Emphasising your noble motives and how you're being punished for them. 'I did absolutely nothing to deserve this'
+ **Villain stories:** Overemphasising the other person's guilt and/or stupidity. Use of damaging and generalised labels is very common, such as: 'That idiot/racist/chauvinist/scumbag caused this'
+ **Helpless stories:** You were driven to act by circumstances out of your control. 'I had no choice. If I'd have told the truth, I'd have been fired'

Example of all three in action: 'I did everything for her [victim], but there was no point [helpless] because she's just a crazy control freak [villain].'

⑤ Learn to challenge your own interpretations of events

Remember: it's not what happens that affects you, it's how you interpret what happens. Start to recognise when you're telling victim, villain or helpless stories and check in with yourself: 'Why do I feel the victim in this drama? Why do I feel helpless? Why is X being such a bully?'

I'm going to wheel out every nanna's favourite cliché here: there are two sides to every story. You only know one side and so the story you're telling yourself is, by its very nature, biased. Acknowledging this will put you in a better mindframe to start a difficult conversation. Trying to understand the other person's side doesn't mean you're saying you'll agree with it. You're not 'giving in' or conceding by getting the full story. You're just getting all the information so you can make an informed decision.

Criticism: how to give it

No one ever wants to be wrong or ridiculed, so people don't take kindly to having their mistakes flagged up. This is why it can work in your favour to flag up your own mistakes first (as mentioned in Chapter 4) and also to re-think how you view criticism. Instead of steaming in with a head full of self-righteous fury, tread carefully, acknowledging that you don't know everything (because you only have your own side of the story). This way it's not criticism, as such, just a process of gaining more information. Viewing it this way will make you calmer and more willing to listen.

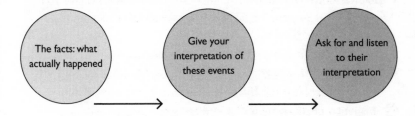

Giving criticism: the dos

+ If something is bothering you, bring it up. Don't just sit on it and indulge your 'flight' tendencies, otherwise you'll feel resentful
+ When stating the case, stick to cold, hard facts rather than emotionally driven labels or opinions. Facts are impossible to argue with. For example: 'You look at my chest when you speak to me' rather than: 'You're a pervert' or: 'You're raising your voice and thumping the desk' rather than: 'You're frightening people'
+ Use conjectural words when stating your interpretation of events, such as, 'I think' and 'It's my opinion that'. There's nothing more off-putting or anger-inducing than someone stating a thought as a fact. For example: 'I feel that you may be underestimating my qualifications' rather than: 'You are underestimating my qualifications'. 'I think' or

'I feel' are not weak or unassertive. You're being honest about how you're stating an opinion not a fact, which will let the other person know that you'll be open to hearing their opinion in turn. Bringing up the subject in the first place is assertive

✦ Use positive words for someone's negative traits: 'You're very passionate and determined', rather than: 'You're a terrifying maniac'. Then state the facts: 'You're very passionate and determined, however, I find it difficult to approach you when you keep jumping down my throat'

✦ Acknowledge that there may be facts they know about that you're not aware of: 'Do you see things differently? Do you know something I don't?'

✦ Listen to their interpretation with an open mind

✦ Be patient and keep looking out for signs of fight or flight. And if this does happen, follow the AMPP rules on page 114–15 to steer the conversation back onto the right track

Giving criticism: the don'ts

✦ Don't use hyperbole: 'He was monstrously unfair and utterly unreasonable'. People will be immediately suspicious of your claims and your genuine concerns will get lost

✦ Don't mistake aggression for assertion

✦ Don't only look for information that backs up your point while dismissing anything that doesn't. This is one of the biggest issues with confirmation bias, where we search for evidence that backs up our beliefs and ignore anything else. Be aware of it

✦ Don't use inflammatory terms: 'That's just disgusting, plain and simple'

✦ Don't succumb to labelling: 'You are sexist'

✦ Don't throw in back-up: 'The CEO agrees with me' or 'Everyone in the family feels the same'. You're making your argument look weak – the facts you've stated and your interpretation of them should be enough without having to summon up the invisible masses to bolster your case. You're also undermining the person you're speaking to by effectively telling them that whatever they say is pointless because everyone's already made up their minds. They will, of course, immediately become defensive when put in this position

✦ Don't make it personal: 'Your father would be ashamed of you'

✦ Don't make generalisations: 'No one else in the company has ever done anything like this'

✦ Don't use disclaimers – they undermine whatever you say: 'Call me crazy, but…', 'I know it's probably not true, but…', 'I'm sorry, but…'

Most importantly, remember that while you're aware of fight or flight triggers in conversations, the person you're speaking to probably isn't. They may state thoughts as facts, they may label people with derogatory words and they may generalise or get personal. Now you're aware of these things, you won't be as affected by them. Stay calm and stick to your new rules.

Example: Driven mad by neighbours

Samantha tells her neighbour, Pete, nicely, not to park in her space. He agrees… but keeps parking there. There are other spaces available for Samantha to park in, but everyone has designated spots and hers is right outside her house. She fumes over it for weeks. Every time she turns into her road her heart races in anticipation of seeing Pete's car in her spot. After a particularly grim day at work, she finally snaps. She blocks his car in, leans out of the window and screams obscenities at his house while shaking her fist. Another neighbour opens their front door and asks, 'What on earth's the

…⟶

....⟩

matter?' Samantha screams: 'Pete keeps parking in my space!' The neighbour looks at her as if she's never heard anything so ridiculous in her life and shuts the door.

The thing is, Samantha's not actually angry at the fact Pete's parking in her space any more, but at the fact that he's doing it after she asked him not to. She feels disrespected and has taken it personally.

A bad conversation:

'Pete – what's wrong with you? You've totally ignored our previous chat. You don't respect me at all. It's unbelievable. All the neighbours agree you're being a complete jerk. I want you to move your car right now.'

A good conversation:

'Hi Pete. I don't mean to sound petty and I hate bringing this up again, but I do really want to be able to park in my space ['do'/'don't' strategy]. It's just easier because it's right outside my house. I often have to carry heavy equipment in from my car and I pay a surcharge for that particular spot [facts]. You have a space allocated to you over there [fact]. I was just wondering why you're still parking in my space after we discussed it last month? [conjectural tone, asking for their interpretation].'

Pete: 'I'm so sorry. I should have spoken to you about it. My wife has had a hip operation and she struggles with the walk to and from our space. It's been so stressful I forgot I hadn't mentioned it. I'll go back to my old spot now.'

Samantha: 'Oh! I had no idea. Of course you can keep using it, then. How long do you think you'll need it for?'

How to deal with criticism when you're on the receiving end

You're not the only one who doesn't like dishing out or receiving criticism, so bear that in mind when someone finds fault with something you've done. If they're being aggressive or seem to be overreacting to a small issue, they're probably nervous about bringing it up or have been stewing about it for weeks and have lost perspective. Now that you're familiar with common conversational patterns you won't be surprised by them and can step back and try to quash your natural desire to defend yourself, thus interrupting the standard Criticism Vicious Circle:

The problems
continue and the
resentment grows
until…

You are criticised

You lash out and
criticise the other
person in turn

You both retreat
into silence

They become
defensive and
aggressive

How to coax others into talking and sharing views

When people react with fight or flight in conversations, don't get angry or frustrated, but accept that they must feel angry, frustrated, scared or insecure themselves. Remember – people aren't usually difficult for no good reason. The way to get them talking effectively is to use AMPP (Ask, Mirror, Paraphrase, Prime):

Ask

And ask sincerely. Good managers, leaders and general conversationalists are genuinely interested in others. If you don't care, people will know and will clam up because what's the point? Ask in a non-threatening and calm manner: 'I'd really like to hear what you have to say', 'I'd love to hear your views on the subject', 'Let me know if you see things differently'.

Mirror

If their body language and tone don't match up to what they're saying, describe this to them in a factual manner (*your* tone and body language are super-important here – they have to be approachable and calm): 'The thing is, you don't look "fine", you look angry and upset. Are you?'

Paraphrase

Once they've told you their interpretation of events, repeat it back to them in your own words. This will help them to assess their own story and give them an opportunity to fill in any factual gaps: 'So, let me just check I've got this right: you're angry because you believe Barbara undermined you in the meeting and you think she's done this more than once?' Be careful that you don't state their version back as if it's factual, so say: 'You're angry because you believe Barbara undermined you' rather than: 'You're angry because Barbara undermined you'.

Prime

If, after all that, you still haven't got anywhere, have a guess: 'Do you think that if X happens then Y might follow? Is that what you're worried about?' Only do this as a last resort as you don't want to put words into the other person's mouth or thoughts into their head, but it can be a very useful tool for convincing people that you do genuinely want to hear what they have to say. If you're right, they may be more tempted to expand on what you've said. And if you're wrong, they may tell you their version just to correct you.

The big BUT: don't push people too hard. It's not *Question Time*. If people aren't ready to talk, they're not ready. If they're in the midst of fight or flight they may need time to calm down. They may recognise in themselves that talking right now wouldn't be such a great idea. Also, if the issue is a big one, you may need to convince them slowly that they can trust you.

Thoughts to take away

✓ Always remember that there are two sides to every story. You don't know everything and people don't usually act like jackasses for no good reason

✓ Always base your point in FACTS first, not hyperbolic opinions or inflammatory statements. No one can argue with facts

✓ Don't avoid awkward or potentially difficult conversations. The success of both our personal and professional lives relies on the conversations we're willing to have – on what we both do and don't say

7

Deal or No Deal

Learn how to bargain, barter and haggle your way to a better deal, whether it's with your boss about that long overdue pay rise or with your neighbours over who's going to pay for the new garden fence.

'And that's my final offer! Hello? HELLO?'

'Negotiating' is an intimidating word, conjuring up images of characterless boardrooms full of angry people in badly fitting suits shouting at each other – something I've never experienced and pray to God I never will. Yet all of us negotiate all the time. In our personal lives we negotiate with estate agents over our rent, with mobile-phone companies over new contracts, with our in-laws over who's hosting Christmas (not me, thank you) and with children over not climbing into the washing machine. And, when it comes to business, we negotiate everything from pay increases, workload, deadlines, promotions and new deals, to who's going to answer the phone this time. Or at least we should. Negotiating is a skill we need to master in order to progress in all aspects of our lives, yet we can avoid it through a lack of confidence ('I'm lucky they want me at all – best not push it'), intimidation ('they're so sure of themselves, they must be right') or a fear of confrontation ('I can't face fighting them'). Well, screw that. Learning to negotiate is an essential tool to succeed in any project. Here are the basic rules to follow so you can face any deal-making situation with aplomb.

Don't avoid negotiating

It's shocking how many people avoid negotiating altogether – even in situations where it's expected. The whole reason you're in a position to even consider negotiating is because you have something the other person wants. That knowledge alone should give you the confidence to have a crack at it. No one is going to be upset by you simply asking for a better deal – as long as you're not aggressive, rude or disrespectful. They can just say no. Negotiating shouldn't be confrontational. If someone is being combative, you can try to calm the situation down using the strategies you learned in Chapter 6 or reassess the relationship you have with them (i.e. is it a long-term or short-term partnership? See next point).

By avoiding negotiating you'll lose out, plus you may appear weak in the eyes of the other party. If you immediately agree to all terms, it's natural for people to think, 'Damn, that was easy – what's wrong with this deal?' For example, imagine you're offered a new job and your boss-to-be says, 'The salary is £60,000 per year'. You say, 'Wonderful! Thanks very much!' The boss breathes a big sigh of relief, but then thinks, 'I was prepared to go to £67,000. Why didn't she negotiate? Is she as good as I think she is? I hope she's going to be able to negotiate contracts favourably in the course of doing her job...' Not only might your new boss question your skills, but think about what you've just lost: £7,000 per year, plus what that's worth in incremental salary increases, pension payments and bonuses. If you don't ask, you don't get.

Is it a long-term or short-term relationship?

Once you've decided to negotiate, work out whether the deal you're trying to strike is with someone you'd like to have a long-term relationship with or if it's a one-off. For example, a long-term relationship might be with a supplier you'd like to keep on contract or a family member you can't simply ignore for the rest of your life (even if it is Creepy Uncle Jeremy). While a short-term, one-off deal could be with the plumber fixing your washing machine. Working this out is key to what happens next...

Know when to play hardball or go for the win-win

If it's a one-off thing, you can afford to be a little stubborn about it. If you're selling your house and are dealing with strangers, you can weigh up how much you want their money with variables such as the time you need to sell by and whether they're in a long chain and then simply say: 'No, thanks' if you believe that's best. You don't need to give a monkey's about what they're getting from the deal, as after this you'll never see or hear from them again. However, if it's someone you intend to know for a while or that you already have a personal relationship with, you always need to think win-win.

Win-win is exactly that: where both parties walk away with something they're (reasonably) happy with. Don't ever go into a negotiating thinking: 'I must crush them!' – they'll smell you a mile off and slam down their defences. This is particularly important if heightened emotions are involved, for example if you feel your reputation's on the line, that you've been treated badly, that you're 'owed' a good deal or if it's personal between the two sides, i.e. in a divorce or custody battle. 'Winning' means the other side must be 'defeated' and unless they're complete fools they'll see that's the outcome you're proposing and won't accept it.' Ayesha Vardag, president of Vardags, the divorce and family law solicitor, explains: 'Strong negotiation means you get what you want and make the other side feel they're getting enough of what they want too, so they buy into the deal'. Win-win means you have to give a little to get a little so a) the deal can be made at all and b) the relationship is treated with respect. If you refuse to negotiate at all on something with your brother, for example, you could potentially damage that relationship for good. You need to put working out a fair deal at the centre of the table – make them think that negotiating with you is in their favour.

Research everything that will come up

Make sure you know everything that's going to be raised in the negotiation and have thoroughly researched it. Don't get wrong-footed by fixating so strongly on one aspect of the deal that you forget about everything else. Imagine you're mentally slapping yourself on the back for signing up a new client when they say: 'Now let's discuss your obligations to our business partner, Gemma,' and you think: 'Who the hell is Gemma?' You're immediately on the back foot and this means the other party can take advantage of your 'ums' and 'ahs' to talk you into a better deal for them. If this happened while you were in the mobile-phone shop, for example, you could leave with a new contract that only costs you £10 per month, but the handset's second-hand, there's no insurance, text messages cost 50p each and you can only access 4G when hanging out of a second-storey window.

Know your priorities, but stay open-minded

Know what your main goal is – i.e. 'I want my friend Rob to move out of our house so my girlfriend can move in' or 'I want to only work four days a week rather than five' – but stay open-minded about what you may consider. As Ayesha explains from experience, it can be counter-productive to think: 'I won't budge on that at all', when there may be options on the table you haven't even considered. For example, your friend may say: 'If you let me stay another two months I'll let you use my car whenever you want', or your boss may say: 'You have to work five days a week, but you can have an extra two weeks' holiday allowance a year'. If you stick stubbornly to what you entered believing was your bottom line, you may miss out on new deals that actually suit you better.

Make your offer first – and be ambitious

Going first in negotiations and being ambitious (even wildly so) will work in your favour. It's all about 'anchoring' (see the box, page 122–23). So ignore thoughts like: 'But if they go first, I'll know where I stand' or 'What if I go too high and look arrogant or go too low and scupper my chances?' Anchoring is proven to work.

What is anchoring?

In one study, half the participants were asked: 'Did Gandhi die before or after the age of nine?' while the other half were asked: 'Did Gandhi die before or after the age of 140?' The first group answered 'around 50', while the second group answered 'around 67'. The 'anchor' numbers of nine and 140, despite both being ludicrous, directly influenced the answers the groups gave, pulling them either lower or higher. 'Anchoring is the cognitive bias that influences us to give much greater weight to the first information we receive', mediation and negotiation expert John Curtis explains. This is why it pays to be ambitious. Even if your offer is fairly outrageous, you anchor that figure in the other party's head and it influences how they view the deal.

Anchoring is enormously influential in our day-to-day lives. 'Imagine you see an item when you're out shopping with a £50 price tag. That's the anchor: the first bit of information we have about this product,' John says. 'If it's 20% off, we automatically think we're "winning". Like it or not, aware of it or not, our minds continually refer back to that £50 price tag. Anything less than that is a deal. We rarely become more objective and ask ourselves: "How much did it cost to produce?", "Could I make one for less?" or "I wonder if I could get it cheaper elsewhere?".'

Here's an example: Lucy wants to get a new website logo designed. Simon wants to design her logo. The absolute maximum Lucy can afford to pay Simon is £500 (her breakpoint). The cheapest Simon can do the job for is £300 (his breakpoint).

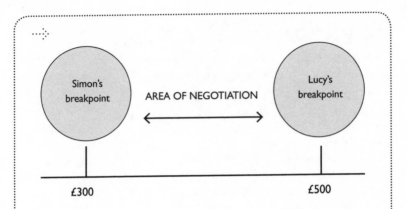

Bearing in mind neither of the parties know the other's breakpoint, whoever goes first here will be in the stronger position because they'll anchor their figure in the other party's mind. So if Lucy goes first and says, 'I can pay £250', Simon will think, 'Wow – I was going to open with £600! That's obviously way too high for her', and, as research has proven, he will likely lower his opening gambit, countering with something like: 'That's too low for me. I could do it for £475'. He's just shaved £125 off what he was originally going to pitch and (he doesn't know this) but he's already below Lucy's breakpoint. She now knows that she's going to get a good deal, while he doesn't, leaving her in the much stronger position. Imagine you're an architect pitching to design someone's house. If you say, 'My usual rate is £20,000, but I'll give you 10% off' even though your usual rate is half that, you haven't only shifted the perceived area of negotiation in your favour, but have added the generosity of a 'deal' on top.

If you can't go first, re-set the anchor

If, for whatever reason, the other party puts forward their proposal first, just re-set the anchor by saying: 'Thanks for your offer. I was thinking more along these lines.' Don't, whatever you do, ask them to justify their offer. They'll defend it as if their life depends on it and the more their figure or proposal will get embedded in both your heads.

Know who you're dealing with

Check references and do some digging – both for one-off negotiations and long-term relationships. If you're hiring a builder for a one-off job you still want to make sure they're trustworthy, just as you would if you were hiring an accountant for the foreseeable future. Not looking someone up online who you're considering making a deal with is unforgiveable nowadays. Plus, you can use what you discover to your advantage. As already discussed in Chapter 4, revealing that you've taken the time and effort to discover more about a person is flattering – it shows you've paid attention and are interested in them. So, before you meet, research both them and their company, look up their Twitter, Instagram and LinkedIn profiles. Have they recently moaned about pot-holes in the road or the cost of car insurance? Are they a keen cyclist? Use this information to create some camaraderie (but not in a creepy way. So, 'I cycled in today and nearly killed myself in a pot-hole! Oh, you've had the same experience? Isn't it infuriating?' rather than, 'I liked that Instagram holiday picture you posted in 2012'). You might even discover something that alters how you feel about the deal or about them as a person. Is the company in trouble? Have they had any bad press? Are they up against any looming deadlines? Be careful how you apply this knowledge (don't blurt it out or make them feel small), but do take it into account.

Don't make meaningless threats or ultimatums

'And that's my final offer!' is a very dangerous thing to say in a negotiation. Because what if it's not? What if you end up backing down? You can't very well say: 'No this is really, truly my final offer. I think', while still looking strong, powerful and in control, can you? Only ever say it if you mean it. But if you do mean it, then walking away can look pretty impressive and give you a reputation as someone who keeps their word (as long as your final offer wasn't dumb or naive).

Don't be over-confident or an ass

Every negotiation is different because people are different. You're dealing with real people possessing real insecurities, foibles, frustrations and personal lives. So no matter how many times you've 'done this before' or how amazing you think you are, the people you're dealing with don't care and, for all you know, might have had a really crap day. So be pleasant, calm and diplomatic (see Chapters 4 and 6). Yes, you can be forthright and determined as long as that doesn't veer into aggression, smugness or intimidation. For example, never whoop with joy when you shake hands on a deal – no one likes to think they've 'lost' or been made to feel stupid. Also don't brag on social media about having just taken someone for a ride (you'd be surprised at how often people do this).

However, don't be too solicitous either

You are there to get a good deal. Whether or not the other person gets a good deal is up to them. Now is not the time to concern yourself over their welfare. You need them to feel that they're getting something out of it to sign up, but whether they actually are or not isn't your problem. (This point obviously varies according to who you're dealing with and whether you have a personal relationship with them. You don't want to take your grandpa to the cleaners.)

Can you deliver what you've promised?

If you can't, don't do the deal. If you suspect that the other party can't, don't do the deal. Take some more time. Try to work around the obstacles to find a new proposal that will work for you all.

'Nothing is agreed until everything is agreed'

This saying is often bandied about in negotiations – and rightly so. It means you should keep note of what has been potentially agreed as you go along, but not sign anything until all the details have been thrashed out. You don't want to get to the end of a two-hour debate only for someone to say, 'Well, an hour and a half ago, you said you'd do X' and realise you've accidentally signed up to teach your neighbour's daughter the clarinet.

Make sure the deal is as agreed when you see it on paper

Scrutinise the contract or letter of agreement and, if necessary, get a lawyer to scrutinise it too. Make sure everything you agreed vocally is included. The era when a handshake was as good as a signature is long gone. Keep any notes or emails so you can prove what was said and when.

If you can't handle it or if it's not appropriate for you to negotiate, then get someone to do it for you

Having someone to negotiate for you can be a blessed relief. It takes away the pressure of self-promotion and of having to be tough – especially in a situation where you already have a relationship with the other person/ company. The agent or lawyer can be pushy on your behalf and emotions stay out of it. Alternatively, designate one of your group to be the 'diplomat' within the negotiations and make it their role to keep things moving, defuse tension, curtail any potentially combative attitudes and to generally be peacemaker – like the host of a political debate.

Some deals aren't worth making

Sometimes you have to be prepared to say no. Don't be so determined to make a deal that you end up with something not worth the paper it's written on.

Thoughts to take away

✓ Don't avoid negotiating. You can miss out on big opportunities (and often more money). If you don't ask, you don't get

✓ Think win-win when it comes to longer-term or personal negotiations. Be open-minded and willing to compromise. Both sides need to feel they're getting something out of the deal

✓ A negotiation isn't an argument. Always enter into one calmly and respectfully. It's the only way to guarantee success (even if you can't make a deal, you'll still leave having learned something – and with some new connections too)

8

Stop Procrastinating and GET ON WITH IT!

Procrastination is kryptonite to success. It slowly withers ambition, making you feel fearful and anxious until just the idea of starting whatever it is you're putting off causes you to break out in hives. Learn how to beat your procrastination tendencies and crack on with confidence. Success will be yours!

The insidious nature of procrastination

'I'll just make a cup of tea and then I'll start – woah! Is that an eagle? Wow, look at the state of those windows. I'll clean them immediately.' It's amazing the excuses we come up with for not starting things. Whether you're putting off phoning your dad, paying a bill or applying for that promotion, avoidance is the default position of the anxious, stressed, fearful and (yes, admit it) the lazy. We can while away days, weeks, months and even years daydreaming about winning that Pulitzer or developing that app, but instead of doing anything about it, we spend our time watching cats in hats on YouTube or working ourselves to the bone in a hellish job we hate.

Procrastinating sometimes is normal. No one is super-efficient all the time. Occasionally we just need to chill out and watch a Scandinavian police drama on TV. However, avoidance becomes a problem when it's stopping you achieving what you want to achieve and when it's making you feel anxious, frustrated, guilty or ashamed. And, when you start battling those emotional demons, whatever you're putting off drifts further and further away and seems less and less achievable. All of which is summed up in the natty little diagram opposite.

Procrastination can be a massive crater in the road to success. But if avoiding things by sticking our fingers in our ears and humming an out-of-tune ditty is so bad for us, why do we do it?

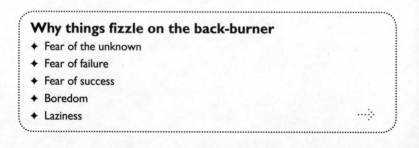

Why things fizzle on the back-burner
+ Fear of the unknown
+ Fear of failure
+ Fear of success
+ Boredom
+ Laziness

⋯

And within those main points live:

- ✦ Anxiety, stress and worry
- ✦ Self-sabotage
- ✦ Low self-esteem
- ✦ A lack of time
- ✦ Fear of judgement and/or rejection ('you're not good enough')
- ✦ Our own judgement ('I'm not good enough')

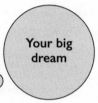

Your big dream

Put off even thinking about your dream

Feel anxious, guilty and ashamed

Distract yourself

Distract yourself some more

Feel pressured and unable to start the task

Ⓢ Make a Procrastination List

1 Make a Procrastination List of things you routinely put off (ensuring you include the Big Dream for success you're currently avoiding like the plague). It doesn't matter how big or small the things are – everything from 'having my sister round for dinner' to 'quitting my job and starting up my own company'. You may think you don't put anything off – that you're steaming through life full-throttle with the wind blowing in your freshly cut hair. If so, congrats: that's great! But it's also very rare. So if you're genuinely not avoiding anything, wonderful. But if you are, write it down. It's important to write it down because seeing it in black and white will make it REAL. And yes, real is terrifying, but terrifying is the kick up the bum you need.

2 When you've got your list, write down next to each thing why you think you're putting it off. And be honest. Use the reasons noted on the previous pages as inspiration.

Side note: If you're wondering why avoiding calling your dad would in any way hinder your route to success, consider this: how often do thoughts like 'Damn! I still haven't called him', or 'I really must speak to him' cross your mind while you're doing other things? How often are those thoughts followed by a pang of guilt? Personal things you've relegated to the 'not important' pile can leap up and punch you on the nose when it's least convenient, putting you off what you're doing and starting a negative emotional spiral. By tackling personal and professional avoidance you'll feel more in control, less stressed and more focused.

Key reasons why we procrastinate

Coming up next are some summations of the key reasons we procrastinate. I asked you to make your Procrastination List before reading these, for reasons soon to become apparent.

Laziness

During a talk I gave on procrastination at Birmingham University, someone asked: 'Why do I put off things that I actually want to do?' Good question. I think most of us have experienced that feeling of secret relief when a friend bails on dinner, someone's leaving drinks are cancelled or your favourite gym class is over-subscribed. It's the relief that comes from knowing you can sit on the sofa in your pants eating beans on toast completely guilt-free. And why do we feel relieved? Because it's always easier NOT to do something.

If your plans involve organising, travelling, concentrating or even thinking (so every plan, then), it's easier simply not to do it. This means that even if you desperately want to apply for that new job or fire that terrible member of staff, it's probably a hell of a lot simpler... not to. Because if you do, then more will be demanded of you. It's cause and effect:

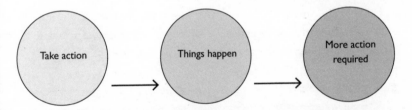

The trouble is: if you never do anything, then nothing ever gets done.

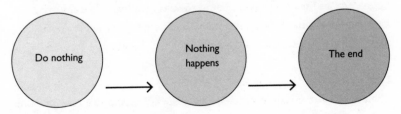

If your quest for success is being held back by pure laziness, with none of the other far more crippling concerns, worries and doubts attached, then you need to get over it and get on with it. No one is going to just give you a new job. No one is going to gift you a life-changing pay rise out of the kindness of their hearts. They're not going to look across a crowded office and go: 'You know who doesn't seem bothered about anything, but really deserves this amazing opportunity? Jeff. Jeff's our guy.' Jeff is one of those people who thinks they can win the lottery even though they don't play – and then resents the people who do win. Don't be like Jeff.

Boredom

Paperwork is boring. Paying bills is boring. Revising for exams is boring. Writing a ten-page job application is boring (particularly when it's full of questions like: 'Give an example of when you resolved conflict within a work environment'). But, the thing is, the task will still be boring when you eventually start it, but, because you've left it to the last minute, it'll then also be stressful, angst-inducing and a million times harder than it would have been had you started when you should have.

Fear of the unknown

This is when those 'worst-case scenarios' rear their gremlin heads and make you wonder: 'What was I thinking? Obviously I can't do this! It'll be the end of life as I know it.' Head back to Chapter 2 for a full explanation of what they are, how they try to convince you they're facts and what to do to beat them.

Fear of failure

What if you fail? Oh the shame! The HORROR. The 'what ifs' have piled up and up and up in your mind until they've blocked out everything else. They're so terrifying that you've lost all sense of reality. Failing is THE END

OF DAYS. The only thing for it is not to do it at all – so you can't fail – or sabotage your own chances, so that at least you can say: 'I only failed because I didn't try'. Great. Brill. High-fives all round.

But let's step back a minute and think about the question seriously: what if you fail? Will the world actually end or could you chalk it up to experience, take what you've learned and try again? You could apply for another job or another course. You could re-book the exam. You could wait for another promotion to come up. You could do better on the next presentation. You could try to win the next award. And the best bit? You probably won't fail at all.

Fear of success

What if you nail whatever you're putting off? What if you get the job? What if you win that contract? What if you ask that person out and they say, 'Hell, yes! What's taken you so long?' The pressure, expectation and additional responsibilities that come with success can be frightening. And people like the status quo. We, as a species, like knowing what to expect. It makes us feel safe. But… isn't that sad? Isn't always staying in your comfort zone boring? Our bodies react to excitement and interest. It's what happens when you say you're 'buzzing'. Not all stress is bad and putting some things off leads to missed opportunities and regret.

All of which can lead to self-sabotage

Procrastination-inspired self-sabotage can take the form of: leaving something until the last-possible moment, not doing it at all, avoiding thinking or talking about it, putting off asking for help, not studying or researching something that would benefit you. Basically – doing something half-assed on purpose because you're scared of failing, scared of succeeding, scared of change or lazy. You do it so you feel more in control of the outcome. When you can't guarantee yourself success (because other people are involved and you can't control them) it can feel like the only control you do have – the only influence you can definitely exert – is to cock things up so that you can fail on your own terms. You can then say to both yourself and others: 'It wasn't as good as it could have been because I rushed it' or: 'I didn't really care anyway' while thinking to yourself: 'Imagine what I could do if I did give myself time – I would be magnificent!'

You kid yourself that you won't feel so bad when you fail this way. But you will. You'll feel resentful: 'I knew it wouldn't work out', and also guilty and ashamed because you know deep down that you messed it up for yourself.

⑤ Re-analyse your Procrastination List

Having run through these reasons, re-analyse your Procrastination List. Can you expand on the reasons why you're putting the things off? Be honest with yourself. It's all too easy chalking it all up to: 'I can't be bothered', without going further and asking why? Once you have your reason you'll be in a better position to start working around it.

⑤ Your procrastination mind map

Fill in a mind map focusing on an ongoing source of procrastination (event) and work through the sections, asking yourself these questions:
+ What form does my procrastination take (behaviour)?
+ What thoughts do I have about whatever it is I'm avoiding?
+ How does my body react when the event pops into my mind?
+ How does it make me feel emotionally?

I have filled out an example opposite to help.

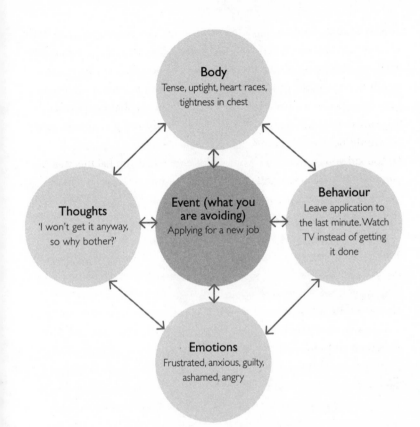

The rollerskating monkey phenomenon

By trying to ignore something, you're just ensuring that you can't think of anything else. For example, if I told you not to, under any circumstances, picture a monkey on rollerskates, what's the first thing that pops into your head? Hello, rollerskating monkey! And now I've put a rollerskating monkey in your mind, you'll see and hear about it everywhere. There'll be a picture of a monkey on an advertising hoarding on your way to work, there'll be a joke about rollerskating on Twitter, someone will ask you 'who do you think will win in a fight: a rollerskating monkey or a skateboarding bear?' (the monkey, obviously). It's similar to when you're trying to avoid someone and you see them on every street corner. Or when you have your heart set on a new pair of trainers and see at least five people wearing them on the bus. It's enough to drive you mad. But the person you're avoiding hasn't got five clones and everyone on the planet hasn't just bought those trainers. You've just altered what you're paying attention to, what you've given priority to in your head. And when you're anxious, that attention is ramped up tenfold because your mind is programmed to focus on 'threats'. By avoiding something, you designate it a threat – as far as your body and mind are concerned, this thing is dangerous. So, if you're avoiding confronting your bullying colleague you'll see and hear them everywhere. You'll overhear conversations about them. You'll get five emails from them. They'll call your mobile. It'll feel as if they've infected every part of your world. And you'll start to feel panicky. Hello fight or flight!

Avoidance is a double-whammy of horror because you also feel guilty and ashamed – on top of panicky. You know you should be doing something about it, so why aren't you? Well, probably because you've put it off for so long it seems like a huge, insurmountable nightmare that gives you heart palpitations every time you think about it. Far easier to just watch those cats on YouTube, right?

So, what's the answer to all this tension, angst and self-chastisement? Well, just thinking about dealing with whatever you're avoiding will deflate your anxiety straight away.

Your anxiety drops as soon as you start facing the problem because humans tend to cope better with things when they know what they're dealing with. When they have a plan. For example, imagine you're stuck down a well. Bad, right? You scream and shout and start to panic. Now imagine you're stuck down a well, but you know your friend has called

Procrastination vs anxiety

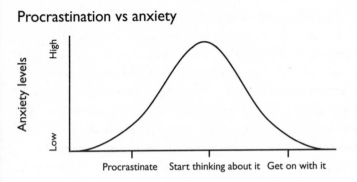

the fire brigade. Better, right? You're still stuck down a well, but you know there's a plan underway to help you, so you're not as anxious. As soon as you start facing what you have to do and therefore know what you're dealing with, your anxiety levels will drop. As Amelia Earhart said: 'The most difficult thing is the decision to act. The rest is merely tenacity.'

⑤ Admit procrastination isn't working as an effective life strategy
Procrastination or avoidance aren't helpful. We can kid ourselves that putting something off or avoiding it helps us to focus on other things or gives us more time to consider the best way to approach the issue. This is rubbish – and admitting it's rubbish is an important step in curbing these tendencies. When you next find yourself dodging a task, ask yourself these questions:

1 Why am I avoiding or putting off whatever it is? What am I scared of? (Refer to your updated Procrastination List on page 136.)
2 Despite your procrastination or avoidance do you still have those fears?
3 If your answer is yes (as it will be), can you accept that putting things off or avoiding thinking about them doesn't solve anything and isn't helpful?

Anti-procrastination strategies

⑤ Set yourself a deadline – and stick to it

Someone who routinely procrastinates will often leave a project until the last-possible moment and then cram all the work into a few hours while weeping and swigging gin. We can all agree that this is a rubbish strategy for success, but, hey, at least the project was started and finished, even if the process was completely miserable – and that's because there was a deadline. You had to do it. One of the reasons you might not be getting anywhere with your grand plan is that there's no deadline. You don't technically have to carry out the plan, and you're not letting anyone else down (other than yourself), so you don't get on with it. The solution to this? Set a self-imposed deadline and stick to it. Also, if you do have a deadline, but it seems ages away and you know you have a habit of leaving things to the last minute, set yourself lots of little deadlines along the way. Here's how:

Start easy

+ Go back to your Procrastination List and put it in order of easiest or most enjoyable things first, through to hardest or least fun
+ Start the first thing. Ticking off something simple will give you a sense of achievement and will motivate you to move onto the trickier stuff

Break down the hard stuff

1 Look at the thing you're most dreading tackling on your list. There it is, thrumming with dark intent, determined to ruin your day. What a monster!
2 Give yourself a metaphorical slap around the face. It's not a monster, it's just a thing! A thing you have to do that you can totally boss. The reason it looks so dark and terrifying is because it's feeding off your angst and

anxiety. Picture it like a balloon that has been swelling up with all your fears and guilt. Pop it! Go on. It'll be such a relief.

3 Make a new list, breaking the one big thing down into smaller steps. So rather than 'write dissertation' put:

 a Brainstorm ideas
 b Go to library to find research books
 c Read some books
 d Write chapter plan
 e Run plan past tutor
 f Start writing chapter 1

 That already looks a hell of a lot less intimidating than 'write dissertation' doesn't it?

4 Once you've noted down all the steps, schedule in a time when you're going to tackle each one. Actually write the deadlines into your diary. You'll be less likely to skip them or dismiss them if they're 'official' and the fact that you've 'booked them in' will cancel out any 'I don't have time' excuses.

5 DO IT. Go through each step during your allocated time slots and if one step throws up something new, add in another part to the plan and bump the deadlines back if needs be.

🅢 Involve somebody else

It's easy to put something off when you're only letting yourself down. We're more likely to do something if other people are involved as we won't want to inconvenience them or admit we haven't done what we promised.

1 Speak to a family member, friend or colleague about your plans and ask them to help. For example, if you want to apply for a new job, tell them that a week on Thursday you're going to show them a list of jobs you're interested in or have them look over your updated CV.

2 Book the time into both your diaries. This will show them that you're serious and they'll feel partly responsible for making sure you do it. Also, you'll feel less likely to blow it off if they've put time aside for you.

⑤ Repeat after me: 'I am not a fortune teller'

You're not. Sorry. Your crystal ball is bunkum. Just because you think something is going to happen doesn't mean that it will (or we'd have all won the lottery by now). By anticipating a disastrous result, you'll behave in ways that will affect the result negatively, thus your fear becomes a self-fulfilling prophecy. You'll self-sabotage by putting the task off until the last minute, not doing it at all, doing it badly, acting aggressively towards other people involved or selling yourself short. And all because you want to avoid a scenario that you made up in your head. Next time a thought pretending to be a fact about the future, such as: 'They'll all realise I'm a fraud' clatters through your head, catch it and shout (in your head or out loud): 'I am not a fortune teller!'

⑤ Am I actually enjoying watching cats in hats on YouTube?

One of the stupidest things about procrastination is that you don't actually enjoy whatever it is you choose to do instead. You can't fully immerse yourself in those YouTube videos and your laughter in the pub is tinged with a hint of hysteria because you know you should be doing something else. The thoughts about whatever it is you're avoiding will encroach on all your other experiences and colour them grey. The next time you're mid-procrastination, ask yourself: 'Am I actually enjoying this?' When you've accepted that the answer will always be 'not fully', you've taken an important first step in owning up to your procrastination and recognising how damaging it is. The next step: DO SOMETHING ABOUT IT.

Thoughts to take away

✓ Procrastination might deliver short-term relief, but will set you up for longer-term angst

✓ Just by starting to think about the issue, your anxiety levels will drop

✓ Admit that procrastination and avoidance aren't effective or helpful strategies – in fact they only hinder and inhibit your path to success

The Producers

To be successful you actually have to do stuff (I know, right?). You have to be organised, productive and creative. You need to learn how to delegate, prioritise and keep things interesting. (But don't worry, I'm not going to advise you get up at 4 a.m. every day.)

Get organised, productive and creative

Proactivity is the key to success. If you don't do anything, nothing happens, ergo you can't be successful. But how do you start getting things done? Confidence plays a big role in productivity. Once you feel brave enough to take chances and to put yourself out there, that's half the battle. Now you also know how to battle your procrastination demons it's time to get organised, productive and creative. If you're organised, you have time and space (literally and metaphorically) to nail your to-do list and to think about things in a more inventive way. Prepare to get stuff done!

Strategies to get organised

It's very hard to concentrate on anything if all you can think is: 'Did I lock the front door?', 'Where's my passport?', 'Did I reply to that text?' Being disorganised wastes a mindblowing amount of time and also money (such as when you have to re-buy the gig tickets you've lost or pay a fine on overdue bills) – it's anathema to success. Getting things sorted is the very first step towards getting things done and while some of these strategies sound simple, they're highly effective. Streamlining your life will make it run more smoothly, so you can concentrate on succeeding at the bigger, more interesting, things.

Ⓢ Make a commitment to get organised

Organisation can be boring. It involves repeating tasks over and over again, day after day, and if you're a fun-loving, spontaneous 'paperwork is dullsville' kind of person, you may rebel against that. Don't. Being organised means you get more done and are less stressed about the chaos in your life. Success on a day-to-day level means feeling confident that you've nailed the boring bits so you can focus on the interesting bits. So the first thing you need to do is make a real commitment to get organised. All of the strategies in this section will take practice so they become new habits. Make them part of your daily routine so rather than chores, they're just something you do, like brushing your teeth or getting dressed.

Ⓢ Make your bed

Always make your bed when you get up. It's an easy win, giving you a sense of achievement first thing and ensuring the place most associated with rest and relaxation will be welcoming for you when you come home.

Ⓢ Open the curtains

Don't stagger around in the dark getting ready in the morning. Your body clock operates according to levels of natural light and opening the curtains will reduce the melatonin (the sleepy hormone) in your system and so make you feel more awake.

Ⓢ Talk yourself through autopilot tasks

Always losing your keys? Can't ever remember if you've fed the cat? We forget everyday things like this because we do them on autopilot while thinking about other stuff, then waste hours worrying about them. You need to snap yourself out of autopilot so your brain registers – and therefore remembers – what you're actually doing and therefore what you've already done. It takes eight seconds to commit a piece of new information to memory, so the next time you're doing whatever it is you usually forget, stop multitasking (or multi-thinking) and talk yourself through the action. Yes, actually tell yourself what you're doing out loud so your brain doesn't only remember doing it, but also hearing about it. You're effectively isolating the event – making it 'special' – from all the other things you do on autopilot. Try it: 'I am putting my keys in the key dish on the mantelpiece'. Adding another factor into the sentence will also boost your memory, so, 'I'm turning off the oven on Monday morning' or 'I'm turning the key in the lock while listening to Spotify'.

Ⓢ Sync your diary with your calendar

You're an adult – update your diary. Those Whatsapp messages asking why everyone's talking about Friday night aren't endearing, they're annoying. Email systems have inbuilt calendars now that sync across your devices. Sign up and you'll immediately feel more in control and on top of things.

Ⓢ Have different notebooks for different things

Have a notebook for work stuff and then a different one for personal stuff. Keep the work one on your desk and the personal one in your bag. This way you won't lose life admin reminders in and amongst work notes and vice versa. Make it a habit to write down all your memos in either book so you don't have to spend 20 minutes searching for a screwed-up post-it note you think you last saw on the floor of your car.

Ⓢ Get an accountant, financial advisor/download a budget app

If you need help managing your money, it's worth spending a little to pass the responsibility onto someone else – or at least to help you think things through and sort out your options. Think of it in terms of money spent versus time and stress saved. Also, consider downloading a budget-making app such as Wally or YNAB (You Need A Budget). Apps like these record your incomings and outgoings and let you know how much you have left to spend. They're great for saving up for specific things, working off a debt or just maintaining a monthly allowance. You're much less likely to splurge spontaneously when you know you'll have to make a record of it.

Ⓢ Get an agent or sign up to a recruitment agency

If you're unsure what you want to do in your working life or are too nervous to self-promote, sign up to an agency who will do the legwork for you. They'll take a commission, but it's a great way to meet new people, experience different working environments and build up your confidence.

⑤ Hire people to do the chores you hate

Hate cleaning? Hire a cleaner. Hate mowing the lawn? Pay the kid next door to make your lawn look pretty. Stop kidding yourself that you're going to do it if you're not, and cut yourself some slack. None of us have super-powers. There are people who do the crap we hate for a living. Hire them and stop feeling guilty about it.

⑤ Download a password manager app

Apps like 1Password generate strong passwords for every login you have and then remember it all for you. It's a digital vault for all the sensitive information you can never remember or can't be bothered to update.

⑤ Tidy your workspace

Some people can work amongst piles of mess, but most can't. You'll know which camp you fall into. If you constantly lose things, find dirt and muck a bit gross and hate that there's no room for your feet amongst all the files and paperwork stashed under your desk, then tidy up. Make a simple filing system for your papers – stuff to do, stuff already done – and bin the rest.

Strategies to get productive

The keys to successful productivity: being focused, determined, unafraid... and not working too hard. Seriously.

⑤ Work fewer hours

A 2014 study by John Pencavel of Stanford University confirmed what many have long suspected: shorter working hours result in better concentration, better mental and physical health, better morale and, therefore, better productivity. When people work longer than 50 hours a week, their output drops; for example, someone working 70 hours a week will produce roughly the same amount of work as someone working 56 hours, meaning that extra 14 hours sitting alone in the office tapping forlornly on your keyboard were a total waste of time.

Ⓢ Give yourself a uniform

Choosing what to wear every morning is a pain in the butt. Introducing a uniform or 'fashion template' to your days will save you both time and money. For example, smart jeans or trousers with a shirt and blazer. Done.

Ⓢ Be willing to say no

Be prepared to say no to things that you don't have time for or that aren't integral to your plans. Don't say yes and then try to cram it in to the detriment of everything else. Focus on your top priorities and the things you've already committed to and say no to the rest.

Ⓢ Use a productivity app on your computer

Often I'll start researching a genuine work query online and 20 minutes later find myself midway through an article called 'How to survive a shark attack'. It's way too easy to get distracted nowadays. Apps like RescueTime let you choose which websites you want to ban or class as 'distracting' and then either blocks you from entering them or monitors how much time you spend on them. It can be a real wake-up call realising how many sites you browse mindlessly and how much time you waste.

Ⓢ Think in terms of days, not years

A study published in *Psychological Science* found that if people framed time in days instead of years, they believed the event to be much closer and therefore more urgent. For example: 'I have 60 days to complete this' rather than 'two months'. When asked when they'd start saving for either college or retirement, participants said they'd save four times sooner when given deadlines of days rather than years.

⑤ Ask for help

This is a big one. People often think that asking for help is a weakness. It's not – it's a strength. The people you think of as most capable are those you trust to speak up when they need a hand, not those who blunder on regardless. When we feel overwhelmed we let our standards slip, forget things and become aggressive or panicky. It ties into our feelings of being a fraud ('I should be able to cope with this; everyone else is') or a failure ('I can't ask for help because people will judge me, fire me or laugh at me'). There are lots of reasons why you might need help. Maybe you've got more on than usual, are being bombarded on all sides or you're doing something that's new to you. Whatever it is, and whatever area of life it relates to (work, family, love, money, health, etc.), just ask for help. Being a martyr, worrier or know-it-all will only bite you in the bum.

Acknowledging you're not super-human, you can't do everything and you don't know everything will feel as if a huge weight has been lifted off your shoulders. And people love being asked for help. They'll feel chuffed that you appreciate their expertise and respect their opinion. A good way to get into the habit of asking is to practise: ask a friend for advice on buying a new computer or ask for directions from your partner. That'll build up your confidence to ask for help for the bigger things.

⑤ Delegate

If you have people to delegate to, then delegate. This goes for your personal life too – if you find yourself doing all the chores, admin or planning at home, share the load. You can't do everything yourself and nor should you want to. People often take everything on through a misguided belief that they're the only ones up to the job, that they're 'meant' to manage it all according to some societal rule, or through a fear of relinquishing control. You need to learn to let go and to trust people to get on with it in their own way.

⑤ Learn to prioritise

1 Write down everything you have to do today.

2 Put the tasks in order of urgency. Which ones need starting today so that you can hit your deadlines? Which will have consequences if they're not done?

3 Next, think in terms of value and importance. How many people are affected by each task? How important is the task to you? How much do you want or need to complete it?

4 Look at your list now and then arrange the tasks in order of least-to-most effort and then start the least first as an easy win to motivate you to move onto the most.

5 Which tasks can you get rid of altogether? When you have lots to do, ironing your pillowcases should be scrubbed off the list. Be strict with yourself. Ask yourself, 'Can I get rid of that?' or 'Is there a quicker way of doing it?' For example, you may want to send thank-you cards to everyone for your birthday presents, but surely you could send out nice emails instead?

⑤ Consider using a stand-up desk

Studies have found that using stand-up desks can hugely increase productivity. Standing provokes a feeling of urgency about the tasks you need to accomplish and so increases concentration. Standing up rather than sitting also improves posture, blood-flow and boosts energy. Many companies will accommodate requests to try one. Why not give it a go?

⑤ Look away from the screen

If you spend all day staring at a computer screen, take short, regular breaks rather than less-frequent, longer breaks. According to a study by Microsoft, our attention spans are getting shorter and your mind can only take in so much information before spluttering out like a soggy sparkler. Leaving your desk, walking around, not checking your phone and having a proper five-minute break will give you impetus to get back to it.

⑤ Don't work hungry

We underestimate how much hunger can affect our behaviour and mood. We, as humans, need to eat. Getting 'hangry' is very real. If you ignore your hunger your body will let you know it's unhappy via various means, ranging in extremity from rumbling noises to cramps and headaches, all accompanied by a dip in mood and energy. A paper published in the *Proceedings of the National Academy of Sciences* reported how the judgements of eight Israeli parole judges varied according to their levels of hunger. The judges would grant around two-thirds of applications at the start of the day, then, as the hours passed, the numbers would fall dramatically, before eventually reaching zero before they were allowed a meal break. After they'd eaten, the approval numbers shot back up before dwindling again, before another meal break was allowed. There were obviously other factors involved in their decision-making, but even when taking those into account, the influence of hunger remained. Hunger makes you grouchy and unable to concentrate. Eat when you need to and you'll be more productive, creative and positive. However, watch out for the dreaded 3 p.m. slump. After a long morning at work, many of us can find our heads dipping closer and closer towards our chests in the mid-afternoon. We feel sluggish, tired and generally a bit 'meh' about everything. One of the ways to beat this is to avoid a carb-heavy lunch. White breads, pastas, potatoes and chips (simple carbs, not made from whole grains), cause a spike in blood sugar followed by a dramatic drop. This is why wolfing a giant jacket potato can leave you feeling slow and drowsy. Having complex carbs instead – wholewheat bread, brown rice, wholegrain pasta – with things like nuts, salmon, yoghurt, spinach, sweet potatoes and seeds should provide you with more energy to last through until dinner.

Strategies to get creative

Being creative means finding innovative ways to think through problems or make new things. It's a unique way of perceiving events, issues or the world in general so you can generate original ideas. You need to be creative to succeed in any challenge. No one got to the top of their game by plodding along, never taking chances and following all the rules. Real life doesn't go in straight lines, so improving your ability to think laterally will inordinately improve your chances of succeeding in whatever it is you're taking on.

Ⓢ Consider writing by hand

Remember the world before computers? You know, Shakespeare, quills and pointy beards? It's time to regress. We've already discussed how writing things down aids memory, but it also prevents the possibility of technological distractions, making you think more deeply about whatever it is you are creating.

Ⓢ Ask for feedback

Don't just carry on doing what you can already do well. It can feel 'safer', but you won't develop your skills or learn new things. And the more you stay 'safe', the more wary/frightened you'll become of taking chances.

Ⓢ Look at problems, obstacles and questions linguistically

In the 1970s, visitors to the Empire State Building complained that the lifts to the top took too long. Engineers discussed: 'How do we make the lifts go faster?' But the lifts were going as fast as was considered safe. A dead-end. But then someone asked: 'How do we make the journey go faster?' This opened up a whole new prospect for innovation. What makes journeys less boring? Distractions. They put floor-to-ceiling mirrors in the lifts, which gave people something to look at and made the lifts appear more spacious. After these had been installed many people commented on how much faster the lifts were, even though the speed hadn't changed at all.

Take a question and work it down to its barest bones – what are you really asking? For example, imagine your tennis club is struggling financially. Someone asks: 'How do we save more money?' and immediately everyone starts thinking of cost-cutting measures, like losing staff members or selling off one of the courts. But the question could just as well be: 'How do we make more money?', which invites much more positive ideas, such as putting on fundraising events, seeking sponsorship from local businesses or hosting a special deal to encourage more members. Examining the words used to describe problems can be a short-cut to lateral thinking. Just re-phrasing the question can give you a new perspective and present a different way of looking at the issue.

⑤ Stop following 'but that's the way it's always been done' mantras

So many people and companies get stuck in ruts because 'that's the way it's always been done'. That doesn't mean it works, though, does it? We often accept inconvenient or sometimes downright stupid rules because we're intimidated by the thought of 'rocking the boat' or we believe that there must be a reason for the rule because otherwise why would it exist? The truth is it probably exists because no one's ever flagged up how inconvenient or stupid it is before, or it suits one person, but not the other 20 who have to go along with it. Stop following these rules. If you always have meetings right before lunch, but no one can concentrate because they're starving, think creatively about how to change things. For example, if suggesting moving it to earlier in the day gets you nowhere, how about ordering food in so you can eat and talk? Not only will the food appease everyone's hunger, but it'll create a more laid-back atmosphere that will encourage brainstorming. Plus, putting the food on the company tab will improve everyone's mood immensely – hell, they'll probably start looking forward to the meetings.

⑤ Keep your brain fresh by stepping out of routines

Breaking up your daily routines keeps your mind ticking over and keeps things interesting. Take a different route to work, go to a different café for lunch, join a different gym class. Mix it up, challenge yourself and you'll find your interest in other things expanding too.

⑤ The three 'whys'

Neil Pavitt interviewed Ricardo Semler, CEO of Brazilian company Semco, for his book *Brainhack*, who told him one way to inspire new ways of thinking is to ask three 'whys' in a row. 'The first "Why?" you always have a good answer for,' Semler explains. 'Then the second "Why?" starts getting difficult to answer. By the third "Why?" you realise that, in fact, you really don't know why you're doing what you're doing.'

⑤ Have a laugh

As already mentioned in Chapter 2, laughing is ridiculously good for you. It not only reduces stress and tension, but also builds a feeling of community and shared experience – essential for building a creative environment both at home and work, so you feel safe to share your ideas and/or ask for help. In an office (and at home) photo walls, doodle chalkboards and desks decorated with personal effects all help to instigate an atmosphere that promotes creativity.

⑤ There are no stupid ideas

We're often held back by our fear of ridicule and so keep quiet when we should speak up. Is there anything more frustrating than having an idea, not saying anything and then hearing it from someone else later on? This is no way to become successful! Remind yourself: there are no such thing as stupid ideas. Ideas are born of ideas. Who knows where your starting point will take you on your road to a successful life?

Thoughts to take away

✓ Be more organised. This will save you so much time, money and angst in the long run

✓ Get productive by prioritising, delegating, asking for help, thinking in terms of days not years and getting rid of unimportant tasks

✓ Embrace creativity in yourself and others. There isn't a single thing in your professional or personal life that couldn't be made more interesting (okay, maybe doing your tax return, but that's it)

10

Work + Play = Success

Slogging away non-stop with no breaks, no variety and only fleeting personal relationships isn't desirable or sustainable. Finding balance in your life is essential to success, keeping you interested, creative and purposeful. 'Don't confuse having a career with having a life,' Hillary Clinton said. Wise words.

It's time to get zen

Those who work relentless 14-hour days, then come home and stare at their emails before passing out fully clothed on their beds are generally not well-rounded, energetic, positive, creative, buzzing people. They're knackered. Becoming over-worked can happen for lots of reasons:

+ Being a workaholic: someone who works to the exclusion of all else and whose thoughts and actions are wholly concerned with their professional lives
+ The competitiveness of the job market. Believing that if you don't work as hard as humanly possible, you'll be overtaken by someone who does
+ The pervasiveness of technology means that you can never 'clock off', as you're expected to be available at all times
+ The blurring of boundaries between the professional and personal on social media, means that you're always in 'work mode'
+ Budget cuts that increase your workload
+ A tyrannical boss who is, let's face it, a controlling slave-driver
+ The threat of redundancies, which makes you feel very insecure about your job
+ If you are freelance, a fear of 'never working again' or 'falling out of favour' with those who you work for

Overworked people are more likely to suffer from anxiety and depression. They're more likely to develop health problems and call in sick. They're more likely to bunk off. They're less efficient. They're less sociable. They're more likely to display narcissistic and perfectionist tendencies. They're more aggressive, snappy, tired, impatient, compulsive and they make mistakes. In short: they're not great to work with – or for.

Nowadays not only is a 'job for life' a quaint idea, it's not even that desirable. The way we work is changing. Companies are adapting to developing markets and technological advancements that advocate flexible working – and so is the workforce. The insecurity of the global economy means there's no such thing as a safe professional bet any more and we're responding to this by widening our skill-sets and looking for success in our personal as well as professional lives. Because, to put it bluntly, no matter how hard you work, shit happens. And if you throw everything into your career and it goes belly-up, you'll be left feeling bereft and unable to cope. However, if you're a well-rounded person with a strong sense of self outside of work as well as in it, you'll be better able to manage set-backs, re-charge your batteries and, if necessary, re-assess your whole position. You need to get some balance in your life if you want to succeed.

Don't get competitive over your spare time

Driven people who constantly strive for success and to better themselves can often get competitive over everything – even their spare time. While this is fine to a certain extent – if you enjoy competitiveness then essentially you are enjoying your downtime – be mindful that everyone else is enjoying it too. When it comes to sports, of course, being competitive makes sense. However, bear in mind that many people play tennis for the fun of it, not to smash the hell out of their opponent. Be wary that competitiveness doesn't spill over into all aspects of your social life and personal relationships. If you start being competitive about who's got the best car or best skiing technique, you'll stop enjoying your spare time, finding it angst-inducing and pressurised, which defeats its entire point.

Technology burn-out

We're 'plugged in' all the time via our phones, computers and tablets. There's an expectation that because we're always accessible we should always be available, so when our boss texts at 10 p.m., we answer. Which, when you think about it logically and fairly, is ludicrous. Listen – it's exceptionally hard to get fired if you are good at your job. If you are conscientious, hardworking (during work hours), skilful, diplomatic and easy to get on with, you will not get fired for clocking off in your own time. And if you are fired for it, you'll have a strong case for wrongful dismissal.

A culture can develop in business where it becomes expected to always be 'on'. But you don't have to sign up to this. Sure, if there's a one-off project, a launch or period of time when you're expected to take on more or stay late, go ahead. But if it's a continuous thing, week after week, month after month, you must restore balance elsewhere or you'll go mad. Your entire life will be work, work, work. Your relationships will suffer – and your work will suffer. You'll feel burned-out and resentful.

⑤ Give yourself tech breaks

Turn your phone/tablet off and shove it in a drawer for at least an hour a day.

We often look at our phones on autopilot for no other reason than because it's there. If someone plonked a bowl of popcorn in front of you, chances are you'd eat it, throwing one piece after another into your mouth without a second thought. Yet if that someone asked: 'Do you want some popcorn?' and you had to think about it, you'd probably say: 'No, thanks. I'm not hungry. Hell, I don't even like popcorn.' Yet, because it's there, you eat it. It's the same with technology. Because the phone is in our hands, we look at it. Even if someone's talking to us, we have a sneaky peek at the screen. Yet, if someone asked: 'Do you want to read a listicle on BuzzFeed right now?' you'd say: 'No, why would I? I'm talking to you.' You have to snap out of autopilot when it comes to technology. By putting your phone or tablet out of reach you'll have to actively *choose* to look at it. You'll have to engage your brain. And making the choice not to will make you feel more in control of your downtime.

This is especially important in today's social media-obsessed world.

There are many businesses that actively encourage interactions via technology rather than getting up and speaking to each other. Millennials (hideous word) are growing up in a world where tweeting about work to colleagues while sitting next to each other is normal. Fine. If that's the way the business works, go with it. But don't be surprised if you get to a point where it all feels a little... much. You don't have to share everything about your life online. You don't have to have an opinion about everything. You can admit you don't know or that you're not bothered. Not everyone needs to hear about what you had for breakfast. Instead of Instagramming pics of Amsterdam, why not go there and enjoy it? Be present. It's far better to say a few things of real value than a whole lot of rubbish. And if you do constantly spew out stuff online, the things of value will get lost. And remember, it's always available for everyone to see. A future boyfriend/girlfriend or boss could look you up and find that offensive tweet from 2012 without breaking a sweat. You can get so caught up in your online life that you lose touch with real life and flesh-and-blood friends. Clocking off for an hour a day will make you feel liberated. Try it.

🅢 Stop. Working. On. Holiday

Unless you are in charge of the nuclear button, the world won't end if you take two weeks off. And if you don't trust that the company won't fall apart without you, you urgently need to reassess your staff or learn to delegate. Don't take your work phone, don't put your mobile number on your out-of-office, log out of your work emails so you can't browse on autopilot – and concentrate on your holiday. If your boss asks: 'When will you be available?' say: 'Sorry, I won't. I need a break. Jess and George are up to date on everything and I trust them implicitly. Also, I'm staying in a remote cabin, which has no telecoms mast within 100 miles, so unless you own a stoical homing pigeon, I won't be contactable.'

Own your commute

The morning commute is a breeding ground for stress: it's monotonous (the same journey day in, day out), you're at the start of a possibly aggravating work day and, most importantly, you have no control over it. You can't do anything about traffic or public-transport issues or the sweaty guy who is standing way too close. This lack of control can make you feel anxious, which can initiate the fight or flight response. When your body's in this state you're more likely to lash out. The best way to regain some control and therefore feel calmer and more positive about the day ahead is to is to own your commute – making the time your own – using the following strategies.

⑤ Make your journey a work-free zone

Yeah sure, super-professionals will brag about how they dictated 15 emails during the drive into work or knocked three things off their to-do list while they cleaned their teeth, but more fool them because they're actually doing unpaid work. Depending on the length of your commute, you're potentially adding hours onto your working day and most probably will enter the office feeling stressed before you've even taken off your coat. Reading the newspaper, listening to music or an audio book, practising mindfulness (check out *This Book Will Make You Mindful* in the same series), doing a puzzle (some mind-game apps have been proven to boost productivity and improve memory), will make you feel as though you're taking control of your commute. You can also tick some things off your SMART-ASS goals lists, for example, by using the time to learn a language or plan your scuba-diving trip. (If your argument against this is: 'I don't have time to waste learning Spanish. I'm swamped with work. I've barely got time to brush my hair', then you need to go back to Chapter 9 and work on prioritisation. There are ways to stop feeling overwhelmed. If it's a case of genuinely having too much to do, you need to speak to your boss about your workload. Don't just battle on. You need balance in your life in order to work effectively.)

Ⓢ Jog or cycle to work

This should appeal to the box-tickers. You're not only exercising, but getting to work and saving money. Tick, tick, tick. It gives you a sense of achievement first thing in the morning, gives you a sense of control over your commute (rather than being held to ransom by train delays or traffic jams), it means you won't be tempted to work because you can't and it's been proven to increase feelings of wellbeing.

Ⓢ Communicate with strangers (I dare you!)

If the train stops suddenly, the bus breaks down or someone starts snoring on your shoulder, share a laugh, a tut, an eye-roll or a concerned grimace with the people around you. It makes you feel less angry, frustrated and less like: 'Why do these annoying things always happen to me?'

Ⓢ Mix it up

Break the monotony by getting off the train or bus a stop early, taking a different route or sharing a lift. Anything to make you feel more in control. This is a good way to get out of your head too – to stop those days when you can't even remember the journey because it's become so routine.

Ⓢ Don't commute

Look into working from home one day a week. Many companies operate flexible working and, if they don't, remind them that perhaps they should. Obviously lots of professions demand your presence (hello surgeons!), but many don't. If you do work from home, though, use the commute time on YOU – don't plonk down at your desk at 7.30 a.m. Instead, go for a run, visit the gym, do some gardening, walk the dog or plan a recipe.

Find meaning outside of work

Exercise, socialise, learn a language, learn to cook, take up life-drawing, start a creative writing course – whatever form it takes, finding meaning outside of work is essential for maintaining a work-life balance. First up, find something you actually want to do.

Ⓢ Your good-time list

Get your notebook out and prepare to make some lists. First up, list the last three occasions when you had a brilliant time with other people. Where were you and who were you with?

A note on working from home

I work from home 90 per cent of the time and I've found following these rules has helped my productivity levels and headspace no end:

+ Create a 'work space' that is separate from where you relax or sleep, otherwise it can feel overwhelming – as if you can never escape from work. The physical act of leaving the room to take a break will give you an emotional break too. (Working on your bed is a bad idea all round – physically and emotionally. You'd be better off finding a local library or café to work in)

+ Get showered and dressed. Don't work in your pyjamas, – you'll feel sluggish and not in 'work mode', no matter how much you blitz through

+ Only clock on at your usual time. Otherwise you'll feel exhausted and out of kilter by midday.

+ Don't feel guilty about enjoying your time. Working at home can feel like a luxury and, as such, you can end up feeling bad for sitting in the garden, going for a walk or having a lunch break. You can actually end up working much longer hours than you would in an office because somehow it's not 'real' work. This is stupid – enjoy it!

Next, list the last three occasions when you had a brilliant time on your own. (Achievement-oriented people can find it hard to relax or enjoy time by themselves. They have to always be 'doing' and measuring themselves against others. Learning to relax and enjoy your own company is an integral part of balance and success. Just say to yourself: 'I'm going to give this 100 per cent' and invest as much energy into it as you do everything else.)

Finally, list three things you've always wanted to start, but never got around to. These aren't things you want to 'succeed' at, just that you think might be fun. You can perhaps use the things you've listed as having been enjoyable for inspiration.

I have filled out some example good-time lists below.

	Good times with other people	Good times on my own	Potential new hobbies
What, when, where and who with?	Last weekend at Michael and Laura's barbecue with all our friends	Last night watching back-to-back episodes of **Veep** on my own	Learn to cook Italian food as that's my favourite.
What, when, where and who with?	Six months ago at Sarah and Steve's wedding with my partner and kids	Last week reading my book in the garden with a glass of wine	Do a creative writing course. I think Katie did one once? Maybe ask her for tips or if she'd like to join too
What, when, where and who with?	On holiday last summer with my dad	Last year, when I went on holiday to Thailand on my own	Learn to scuba-dive or windsurf. Maybe book a holiday purely for that purpose

⑤ Initiate socialising and say yes to invitations

If you like hanging out with Josh, then for God's sake hang out with Josh. Don't wait for him to call you – call him and book something in. We can let pride get in the way of friendships. A fear of rejection and a sense of desperation can put us off making the first move. Loneliness is a bigger problem than ever before in this society of online 'friends' and connections. Real contact has never been so important. Personal relationships with friends or family protect against loneliness, isolation, anxiety and depression. Join a club, say yes to invitations or look online to find local events. Try www.meetup.com if you'd like to meet new people. It's an international organisation that sets up events purely for that purpose.

⑤ Exercise

Exercise makes you feel better physically and emotionally – that's a fact. It also burns off excess energy and is a great way to relieve stress. Plus it's something you can do with other people, making it a social occasion. If you join a team or regularly attend a class it means you're less likely to skip it in favour of work.

Consider exercising outdoors. A study by the mental health charity MIND discovered that people who regularly took a walk outside felt less stressed and reported feeling better all round than those who wandered through a shopping mall. Go figure. So get outside. Do some gardening, take the dog for a walk, have a jog.

Also, take a walk for no reason. Don't always make a plan to get from A to B. Just walk. Having no set destination and no set 'reason' for walking is liberating. It's walking for walking's sake – something we very rarely do in our manic do-everything-now lives. It's strangely peaceful.

⑤ Don't multitask

You can't do it. No one can. No, you're not the exception. Why do five things adequately when you could do one thing brilliantly? And, in your downtime, that one thing is likely to be hanging out with your family, your kids, or spending some time on yourself. You need to give 100 per cent of your attention to whatever you're doing, otherwise you'll miss out. Channel equal amounts of energy into every part of your life and you'll reap the rewards. Be present in the moment and savour these rewards. For that is what success is: feeling fulfilled.

Thoughts to take away

✓ Invest as much time and energy into your spare time as your work time. It'll benefit both and will lead to success all round

✓ Give yourself daily tech breaks. You'll feel calmer realising the world won't end if you put down your damn phone every once in a while

✓ Put aside time for the things you enjoy outside working life. This is just as integral to success as working hard. It'll make you feel energised, interested and creative

A final message

Wahoo! It's round-up time. You've made it to the end, hopefully feeling much more confident about knowing what you want to achieve and how you're going to go about achieving it. The very act of picking up this book and reaching this point means that you're determined to both find and maintain success in your life and that's the first and biggest step to reaching your goals. Many people trudge on in unfulfilling lives – both professionally and personally – because they're scared of making changes, rocking the boat or of failing. Hopefully by now you realise that making changes, rocking the boat *and* failing are all necessary steps on the road to success. It keeps you interested, productive, creative and present in the moment. It means you're not just waiting for things to get better, you're actively working towards it. And for that you should be proud. Putting yourself out there and taking chances can be terrifying, but the rewards are huge. It takes courage to fight for something and also to accept that you may need to change your behaviour and thought processes to get there.

As a means to measure what you've learned, please answer the following questions:

1 After reading this book how do you feel?

A Determined to see my plans through

B Inspired to think more about what I really want

C Surprised at discovering some things about myself that I didn't know

D Dispirited and uninspired – what a load of hogwash!

If you answered A–C, hurrah! That is great news. If this book prompts you to think more deeply about what you want in life and how you might go about getting it, that is a wonderful jumping-off point to start considering your next move. Keep doing what you're doing. You'd be amazed how so much of success boils down to determination, grit and not being a jerk. If you can master those three things then you are well on your way. If you answered D, fair enough, but have you truly given the strategies a shot? Have you honestly put your own behaviour and thought processes under the microscope? Are you letting a fear of failure or change make you dismiss your chances and/or the strategies?

2 **Are you going to work on being more approachable, influential and persuasive?**

Many of the tools in this book are proven to make you more approachable and more influential. While you may secure professional success by being a ruthless egomaniac who cares nothing for anyone else (and certain businesses in certain situations do demand a boss like that occasionally), those cases are rare – and they're very lonely. If you try to take those traits home with you, home is going to be a cold, dark place. Being genuinely interested in other people, doing your research and owning up to your mistakes will make you a lot of friends in the right places.

3 **Do you feel confident in dealing with difficult conversations?**

Don't avoid them – that only leads to recrimination, frustration, missed opportunities and regret. Remember, you can be both candid *and* kind. There doesn't always have to be a 'confrontation' or 'argument' when something goes wrong. There are simple ways to create a safe space for open dialogue, where, as long as everyone feels they're being listened to, you can douse anger and fear and have a helpful, useful conversation.

4 **Do you feel better able to deal with stress?**

Being able to recognise your own personal response to stress will make you better able to cope with high-pressured situations. However, if you feel that anxiety is deeply affecting your life and you need further help, please speak to your doctor.

5 **Will you feel more confident negotiating?**

Whether it's with your boss, a new client or your family, knowing how to negotiate fairly and effectively is an essential life tool. Practise the strategies in non-pressured situations (like at the local market or with your kids) so you feel better prepared for when the stakes are higher.

6 **Will you be more aware of your procrastination tendencies?**
Procrastinating is short-term gain for long-term pain. You're just ensuring that your anxiety about the project festers and grows. Just thinking about starting it will reduce the angst.

7 **Are you going to get more organised, productive and creative?**
It is possible to be all three of these things. Learning to manage your time effectively will give you the headspace to get things done and think about things in original and inventive ways.

8 **Are you going to work towards a meaningful work-life balance?**
Having balance in our lives is essential for finding meaning and for feeling fulfilled. Without balance both our work and personal lives suffer. To truly feel successful you need to invest as much energy and time into both.

9 **What 'thoughts to take away' struck a chord?**
Write them in your notebook and refer back to them whenever you hit a rough patch or need some inspiration.

10 **When are you going to put all of this into action?**
Look back over the SMART-ASS goals you made at the beginning of this process. How do you feel about them now? Have any of them changed? How many of the stages have you ticked off? If none, when are you going to start? If you're already well on your way, congratulations!

These questions aren't meant to stress you out, but rather to give you a sense of direction. Just skim-reading the book and thinking: 'I'll do it tomorrow' or 'Yeah sure, I know I'm the greatest already', isn't very helpful. We can all improve certain aspects of our lives. If you recognise any of the negative traits detailed in the chapters, why not try the strategies to see if they work? What do you have to lose? You have to start learning to acknowledge when pride, arrogance or fear are stopping you from taking chances and making changes and also learn to recognise when you're making victim, villain or helpless stories to excuse your apathy or negative behaviour. The only person you can control is yourself, so be open and honest in where things might be falling short and go for it.

Success is fluid and things change. Don't be scared to alter and amend your plans according to your own desires and situation. Having a 'great life plan' is all very well, but things often don't go to plan and being flexible and admitting you need to shake things up is an important part of feeling happy and excited about what you're doing. Plodding on regardless because it's 'part of the plan', even if it's making you miserable, is an awful idea. Making changes is frightening, but exciting. Being proactive will make life brighter and more vivid. You have choices – be bold, be determined and make them count!

Success means different things to different people at different times. Be courteous, polite, determined, resourceful, focused and hardworking and you'll find your own version of success in your life.

Good luck!

Further reading

Gillian Butler, *Overcoming Social Anxiety and Shyness* (Constable & Robinson, 2008)

Susan Jeffers, *Feel the Fear and Do It Anyway* (Random House Group, 2012 edition)

Sarah Knight, *The Life-Changing Magic of Not Giving a F**k* (Quercus, 2015)

Natalie Reynolds, *We Have a Deal: How to Negotiate with Intelligence, Flexibility and Power* (Icon Books, 2016)

Useful websites

TED talks: www.ted.com

Forbes: www.forbes.com

LinkedIn: www.linkedin.com

XMind: www.xmind.net

Medium: www.medium.com

Be Mindful: www.bemindful.co.uk

Headspace: www.headspace.com

Gorkana Media Database: www.gorkana.com

ExecuNet (executive network): www.execunet.com

Institute of Directors: www.iod.com

Brightidea: www.brightidea.com

Kickstarter: www.kickstarter.com

Women in Business Network: www.wibn.co.uk

Twitter: www.twitter.com

Meetup: www.meetup.com

It's Nice That: www.itsnicethat.com

References

P.16: Richard St. John, *8 To Be Great: The 8 Traits Successful People Have In Common* (Train of Thought Arts, 2nd edition, 2010)

P.36: Oliver Burkeman, 'This column will change your life: do you feel like a fraud?' (theguardian.com, 2013)

P.48: William Hanson, *The Bluffer's Guide to Etiquette* (Bluffer's, 2014)

P.54: Advice from Nancy Collamer, author of *Second-Act Careers* (Ten Speed Press, 2013)

PP. 68 & 72: Dale Carnegie, *How to Win Friends and Influence People* (Random House Group, 2012 edition)

P. 76: Danny Dyer, *The World According to Danny Dyer: Life Lessons from the East End* (Quercus, 2015)

Chapter 6: Several strategies in this chapter are inspired and informed by the brilliant *Crucial Conversations: Tools for Talking When Stakes Are High*, by Kerry Patterson, Joseph Grenny, Ron McMillan and Al Switzler (McGraw-Hill Education, 2nd edition, 2011)

P.88: Lilias Folan, www.liliasyoga.com

P.156: Neil Pavitt, *Brainhack: Tips and Tricks to Unleash Your Brain's Full Potential* (Wiley, 2016)

Acknowledgements

I'd like to say a massive 'THANK YOU!' to everyone who supported me through the writing of this book. A whole heap of gratitude is owed to my family and friends, most particularly my husband, Ben, who didn't moan (too much) when my paperwork and cold cups of tea took over the living room. To all the therapists, authors, coaches and experts who gave their time, advice and expertise so willingly. To Jane Sturrock, Natasha Hodgson, Charlotte Fry and Alainna Hadjigeorgiou at Quercus for their unfaltering enthusiasm. To my agent Jane Graham Maw for her unwavering support. And to Jo Godfrey Wood and Peggy Sadler at Bookworx for their brilliant editing and design skills. Thanks to Anna Rader for proofreading.

About the author

Jo Usmar is the author of *This Book Will Make You Fearless* and the co-author of six other titles in the *This Book Will Make You* series.

Through her work as a journalist for magazines, newspapers and websites including *The Telegraph*, *Huffington Post*, *Stylist*, *ShortList*, *Glamour*, *Cosmopolitan*, the Mirror and *Look*, Jo is well known for her entertaining tone and light touch with tricky subjects. She has appeared on Radio 4's *Woman's Hour* and *Sky News* discussing her work and is the founder of the Instagram self-help vlog project *Bite Sized Psych*.

www.jousmar.com

ALSO AVAILABLE

 Fearless Feel Beautiful Sleep

 Calm Happy

 Confident Mindful

Quercus
www.quercusbooks.co.uk